P9-EEU-810

UPTON SINCLAIR

Literature and Life Series
[Formerly Modern Literature
and World Dramatists]

Selected list of titles:

Complete list of titles in the series available from publisher on request.

UPTON SINCLAIR

Jon A. Yoder

Frederick Ungar Publishing Co.
New York

Copyright © 1975 by Frederick Ungar Publishing Co., Inc.
Printed in the United States of America
Designed by Anita Duncan

Grateful acknowledgment is made to David Sinclair for permission to quote from the letters, manuscripts, and publications of his father.

First paperback edition, 1984

Library of Congress Cataloging in Publication Data

Yoder, Jon A   1943-
  Upton Sinclair.

  (Modern literature monographs)
  Bibliography: p.
  Includes index.
  1. Sinclair, Upton Beall, 1878–1968.
PS3537.I85Z95   813'.5'2   74–78450
ISBN 0-8044-2989-8 (cloth)
ISBN 0-8044-6998-9 (pbk.)

Contents

Chronology

1878: Upton Beall Sinclair, Jr. is born on 20 September in Baltimore, Maryland.

1888: Moves with family to New York City.

1892: Enters College of the City of New York.

1897: Writes "half-dime" novels to finance education at Columbia University.

1900: Marries Meta H. Fuller in New York City.

1901: *Springtime and Harvest* is published. A son, David, is born in December.

1903: *The Journal of Arthur Stirling* is published.

1904: *Manassas* is published. Goes to Chicago to research *The Jungle*.

1905: Founds Intercollegiate Socialist Society.

1906: *The Jungle* is published. Founds Helicon Hall.

1909: Meets Mary Craig Kimbrough at health resort.

1911: *Love's Pilgrimage* is published.

1912: Divorces Meta in Amsterdam.

1913: Marries Mary Craig Kimbrough in Virginia.

1914: Serves two days for demonstration.

1915: Moves to California.

1917: *King Coal* is published. Resigns from Socialist party.

1918: *The Profits of Religion* is published. *Upton Sinclair's* is begun.

1919: *Jimmie Higgins* is published.

1920: *The Brass Check* and *100%* are published.

1923: *The Goose-step* is published.

1924: *The Goslings* is published.

1925: *Mammonart* is published.

1927: *Oil!* is published.

1928: *Boston* is published.

1930: *Mental Radio* is published.

1932: *American Outpost* is published.

1933: *Upton Sinclair Presents William Fox* and *I, Governor of California* are published.

1934: Wins Democratic nomination for Governor of California; loses election.

1935: *I, Candidate for Governor* is published.

1936: *Co-Op* is published.

1937: *The Flivver King* is published.

1940: Begins Lanny Budd series with *World's End*.

1941: *Between Two Worlds* is published.

1942: *Dragon's Teeth*, winner of Pulitzer Prize, is published.

1943: *Wide Is the Gate* is published.

1944: *Presidential Agent* is published.

1945: *Dragon Harvest* is published.

1946: *A World to Win* is published.

1947: *Presidential Mission* is published.

1948: *One Clear Call* is published.

1949: *O Shepherd, Speak!* is published.

1953: *The Return of Lanny Budd* is published.

1956: *The Cup of Fury* is published.

1957: *Southern Belle*, by Mary Craig Sinclair, is published.

1960: *My Lifetime in Letters* is published.

1961: Mary Craig Sinclair dies, at age 78, on 26 April. Marries Mary Hard on 15 October in Milwaukee.

1962:   *The Autobiography of Upton Sinclair* is published.
1967:   Mary Sinclair dies, at age 85, on 18 December.
1968:   Dies 25 November at nursing home in New Jersey.

The Problem

I saw a man pursuing the horizon;
Round and round they sped.
I was disturbed at this;
I accosted the man.

"It is futile," I said,
"You can never—"
"You lie," he cried,
And ran on.

—Stephen Crane

According to Edmund Wilson, "Practically alone among the American writers of his generation, he [Upton Sinclair] put to the American public the fundamental questions raised by capitalism in such a way that they could not escape them."[1] To Sir Arthur Conan Doyle, Upton Sinclair was "one of the greatest novelists in the world, the Zola of America."[2] To Albert Einstein, Sinclair was "one of the sharpest observers of our time."[3] Few twentieth-century men of letters could compile a list of enthusiastic admirers of higher caliber than those who corresponded with Sinclair. Among them were Sinclair Lewis, Jack London, Thomas Mann, Lincoln Steffens, Bertrand Russell, George Bernard Shaw, Maksim Gorky, Romain Rolland, Louis Untermeyer, Luther Burbank, Floyd Dell, Eugene Debs, John Dewey, Edwin Markham, Edgar Lee Masters, Oswald Garrison Villard, H. L. Mencken, Eugene O'Neill, H. G. Wells, Radindranath Tagore, Charles Fulton Oursler, Norman Thomas, Clarence Darrow, D. H. Lawrence, Maurice Maeterlinck, and M. K. Gandhi.

Obviously, not all of these people agreed with every position taken by Sinclair. But they did have high respect for his skill as a writer, and they considered Sinclair an articulate and intellectual proponent of a respectable point of view. I stress the earlier widespread acceptance of Sinclair because of his currently low status. He is almost completely ignored by American academicians. To the extent that he is considered at all, general evaluation of Sinclair, at least in America, would come quite close to George Orwell's bored conclusion that Sinclair was a "dull, empty windbag."[4]

For most of us, Sinclair has been reduced to the muckraker who described how capitalist meatpackers turned Lithuanians into lard. This problem is presumed to have been solved by laws passed during Theodore Roosevelt's administration demanding federal inspection of meat. Some students of American history retain vague memories of Sinclair's scheme to end the great depression of the 1930s, at least in California, through the application of "industrial democracy." But another Roosevelt was in the White House, and gubernatorial solutions less socialistic proved to be more popular. So much for Upton Sinclair.

There are two reasons, I believe, for the meager reputation of one of America's most significant writers. Sinclair was a socialist. For most Americans, this puts him into the camp of the cranks—interesting, perhaps, but not worthy of serious consideration by those born into the land of the free and the home of the self-made man. Secondly, Sinclair's writings do not meet current academic literary standards. As long as a writer is coming out with work that sells widely on the popular market, that writer's reputation in America is largely in the hands of book reviewers and journalists. But after the writer's death, the primary custodians of that reputation are academicians. While it is difficult to make useful generalizations about American professors, Sinclair's socialism does not seem to be his major liability in terms of getting favorable handling from the academic community. Two secondary problems emerge. Sinclair is hard to administer, and he is not hard to understand.

Truth, in American universities, is usually dispensed by departments. Since few great writers wrote with this organizational principle in mind, squabbles often result. Is Plato the property of the Philosophy Department or the Political Science Department? But working relationships have evolved. The historians may "teach" Harriet Beecher Stowe in exchange for Henry Adams, who has been adopted by English Departments. But how does one administer Upton Sinclair?

His most important novels—including *The Jungle*,

Oil!, *Boston*, and the Lanny Budd series—are as subject
to the territorial prerogatives of Political Science, History, Sociology, and Economics Departments, as they
are to those of the English Department. And the amazing scope of Sinclair's oeuvre is demonstrated by his
work in Medical Arts (*Good Health and How We Won
It, The Fasting Cure*), Business (*The Flivver King,
Money Writes*), Education (*The Goose-step, The Goslings*), Religion (*The Profits of Religion, What God
Means to Me, A Personal Jesus*), Philosophy (*The Book
of Life*), Psychology (*Mental Radio*), and Journalism
(*The Brass Check*). In an age of specialization, Sinclair
attempted to be the Renaissance Man who had discovered socialism.

It could be argued, however, that Sinclair wrote
widely without writing anything worth remembering.
Those who have been dignified with doctorates, regard-
less of specific label, have generally been taught to chant
in unison: "Death to the simple-minded." Thus Granville Hicks—who had, himself, written an analysis of the
1920s in America without considering *Oil!* or *Boston*—
correctly notes that Sinclair "has been either dismissed
or patronized by the majority of critics and literary historians."[5] A typically modern world view perceives the
individual discovering his helpless state within general
chaos. Angst, not an answer, is the respectable response,
and Sinclair is full of simple solutions.

Moreover, those solutions are repeated hundreds of
times in his writings, in ways that cannot possibly be
misunderstood. Consequently, as Hicks observes, Sinclair "does not exist for the serious critics, especially the
younger ones—those nourished on seven types of ambi-
guity."[6] For Malcolm Cowley, to read Sinclair is to "feel
dull and slightly uplifted, as if the editorial page of an
old-fashioned Socialist newspaper had been rewritten in

terms of action and dialogue, but without being dramatized."[7] Even J. D. Koerner, who considers the "omission of Upton Sinclair from a discussion of twentieth-
century literature, especially the literature of dissent
. . . as embarrassing as it is unjustified," concedes that
Sinclair "does not approach the higher levels of creative
literature."[8]

Still other explanations for neglect of Sinclair are
available. Floyd Dell, Sinclair's friend and biographer,
ascribed the problem to the prophet's traditional inability to gain appreciation in his own country: "Americans
generally are truly surprised and puzzled by Upton Sinclair's fame abroad—by the fact that he seems to be
regarded throughout the world as his country's most
distinguished literary figure."[9] But *Time* answered Dell's
contention with chauvinistic clarity: "Of living U.S.
writers he has been far and away the most widely translated—into at least 47 languages in 39 countries. . . .
This is not merely because Sinclair's clear, unsubtle writing practically translates itself. It is because his fables
make social injustice seem simple."[10] Foreigners, we
are invited to believe, honor Sinclair because they like
easy answers.

Others have looked toward Sinclair's genre as the
explanation for artistic failure. According to George
Becker, "Sinclair is first and foremost an historian, a
chronicler of society as it is. However, the reader soon
discovers that in his effort to explain events in terms
which he considers meaningful, the author is bound to
oversimplify, and that the ingredients of his novels
become tiresomely predictable."[11]

And Irving Howe, who has taken a special interest
in political novels in general, contends that the very
attempt to have fiction carry the freight of political ideology automatically encounters theoretical difficulty:

The novel deals with moral sentiments, with passions and emotions; it tries, above all, to capture the quality of concrete experience. Ideology, however, is abstract, as it must be, and therefore likely to be recalcitrant whenever an attempt is made to incorporate it into the novel's stream of sensuous impression. The conflict is inescapable: the novel tries to confront experience in its immediacy and closeness, while ideology is by nature general and inclusive.

But Howe goes on to develop a position that can be used to support a positive analysis of Sinclair:

Yet it is precisely from this conflict that the political novel gains its interest and takes on the aura of high drama. For merely to say that an ideology is, in some sense, a burden or an impediment in a novel is not yet to specify its uses— is not yet to tell us whether the impediment may be valuable in forcing upon the novelist a concentration of those resources that are needed to overcome it.[12]

In terms of defense of Sinclair, however, George Bernard Shaw's attempt to influence the Nobel Prize Committee in 1931 probably comes closest to Sinclair's own point of view. Shaw believed that this international honor should be awarded to

writers whose positions are so far outstanding that it will be recognized internationally; and such positions are not attained by pleasing the professors. They are never purely literary positions: writers who are great pets in literary circles, and perhaps do exquisite literary work, may have no influence on the thought of their time; whilst rougher talents, exercised forcibly by writers to whom literary graces are not ends in themselves but only bait to catch readers for their ideas, may have just the sort of importance that maintains the Nobel prestige. It is because Mr. Upton Sinclair's talent is of this order that I joined in his nomination as eligible for the prize, and that the professors shrieked with horror at the suggestion.[13]

Sinclair, who had slight respect for academicians, had a gigantic, though genial, appreciation of his own endeavors. In a letter published by *Time* (11 October 1948), he cheerfully wrote: "Nobody has ever pointed out any historical errors in the Lanny books, and I will venture to put on record the prediction that students in high schools will be learning their history of the first and second World Wars from these books long after *Time* has ceased to be."

Those who consider Sinclair insignificant base their rejection upon aesthetic criteria, whereas Sinclair was concerned with the effect of his writings upon his audience—a very different matter. As M. H. Abrams has made graphically clear, theories of art deal with the relationships concerning the work itself (an artifact), the artist, the audience, and the universe. "Although any reasonably adequate theory takes some account of all four elements," writes Abrams, "almost all theories . . . exhibit a discernible orientation toward one only."[14] Upton Sinclair, obviously, falls into the category Abrams labels "pragmatic." This means that as an artist he "looks at the work chiefly as a means to an end. . . . The central tendency . . . is . . . to derive the norms of the poetic art and canons of critical appraisal from the needs and legitimate demands of the audience."[15]

Sinclair, then, simply took one of four optional critical stances. He could have been primarily interested in the universe, in which case he would have endeavored "to hold the mirror up to nature." He could have felt strongly the romantic impulse toward self-expression, concerning himself with himself as an artist. Or he could have been interested in the work itself, joining the fondlers of metaphor.

Had he chosen either of the last two approaches and then been as successful as he was within the orientation he pursued so consistently, his critical acclaim would now be enormous. This is to say that Sinclair succeeded, but within a context currently—but not always—unpopular within American literary circles. His approach was old-fashioned, and during a time when the quality of a novel was often measured by its complexity (Faulkner, Joyce), Sinclair's emphasis upon uncluttered communication brought him into conflict with artists whom he respected and journals that shared his political perspective. Writing to William Carlos Williams (16 October 1951), Sinclair stated simply his simple thesis:

Of course every poet is free to write what he pleases, so is every human being; but the purpose of all writing is to communicate with other people, and if a poet writes in such a way as to make his communication difficult, it seems to me that the poet is demonstrably mistaken. . . . I may be left with high esteem for that poet as a man, but I cannot read him as a poet.

Sinclair was particularly annoyed that publications that he felt should be joining wholeheartedly in his efforts to communicate tended to turn down his proposed contributions in favor of more "modern" art. For example, he wrote a poem inspired by the death of Franklin D. Roosevelt that he eventually had to publish as part of *O Shepherd, Speak!* because it did not meet the standards of the liberal weeklies:

> The shepherd is dead, and the sheep
>   Wander alone in the hills;
> The night comes on, the black night,
>   And the heart with terror fills.
>
> The wolves slink in the shadows,
>   They who must be fed;
> Their breath is hot and panting,
>   They know that the shepherd is dead.

> Oh, sorrow beyond telling!
>   Oh, sheep that none can save!
> Oh, heartbreak of the future!
>   O Shepherd, speak from the grave!

As revealed in his correspondence, so far as Sinclair was concerned, there were only two possible explanations for this poem's difficulty in finding a publisher: "Of course the big circulation magazines wouldn't publish anything in favor of Roosevelt, and the *Nation* and *New Republic* never publish any poetry that anybody can understand."

In a letter to the editor of the *New Republic* (5 July 1946) complaining about treatment received from its reviewer, Sinclair contended that it was not he who had the simplistic perspective:

How many persons there are who acquire humane ideas— liberal, progressive, radical, whatever you choose to call them—in the fields of economics and politics and yet remain in the fields of literature and esthetics completely snobbish, antisocial, and reactionary. To say that a book is popular is to make it suspect, and if lines of poetry are written which contain any meaning for the average man those lines are automatically condemned. For the most part these persons have no idea of the watertight compartments in their minds.

Writers who use literature as a weapon for their causes are usually called propagandists—a label that most academic departments affix deprecatingly. But Sinclair's frustration at being scorned from lofty literary positions did not stem from a refusal on his part to accept this label. Unfortunately, although he had written a whole book on literary theory, *Mammonart* (1925), he could not get the literati to concede that:

There are two kinds of propaganda, those which we accept readily and take for granted, and that which is new and strange. The former kind we accept readily as art, and the latter kind we resent and call tendential.

In *Mammonart* Sinclair contends that a proper definition of propaganda does not include negative connotations. To propagandize is simply to make systematic efforts to obtain support for one's own point of view. Thus Sinclair's definition of art represents a minority opinion within modern academia: *"Art is play, to the extent that it is instinctive; it is propaganda when it becomes mature and conscious."* So *The Scarlet Letter* is discussed by Sinclair in terms of the ethics of marriage, and Dante's *Inferno* is described as "The Muckraker's Hell." Since great art, in Sinclair's opinion, *"is produced when propaganda of vitality and importance is put across with technical competence,"* it becomes important to know what Sinclair meant by technical competence and what sort of propaganda he judged to be vital and important. Fortunately, the task is simplified because Sinclair was a remarkably consistent writer in terms of both method and ideological content.

Remembering his audience-oriented goals, it is to be expected that in writing novels that attempt to be informative in a factual sense as well as formative in an ideological sense Sinclair would have problems that do not confront the conventional novelist. To insure the latter goal, Sinclair used obvious ideological spokesmen whom he caused to spread the gospel according to Sinclair. With regard to factual accuracy, he accepted some of the laborious techniques of naturalistic writers. In the *Saturday Review of Literature* (13 August 1949) he wrote:

As a historian I am responsible to my readers for the accuracy of what I give them, and on this point I state that I have tried as hard as I know now to get the facts exactly right. I must

have written a thousand letters to persons who were eye witnesses of this or that scene, or who had had access to inside
information. Thus, in the case of "O Shepherd, Speak!" General Groves read the chapter dealing with the New Mexico
bomb test, Robert Sherwood read the chapter dealing with
Roosevelt's death, and Thomas C. Howe, Jr., director of the
Palace of the Legion of Honor, the art museum of San
Francisco, read all the pages dealing with the work of his
"Monuments" group in Europe. . . . Not an error of importance has ever been pointed out by any critic or correspond-
ent.

When Sinclair claimed to have written letters by the
thousands he was not exaggerating. These letters range
in importance from correspondence with Einstein and
Oppenheimer about the development of the atomic
bomb to the specific clarification of whether or not a
poor family would be likely to sleep on a particular sort
of bed. In addition to providing documentation, Sinclair
used correspondence as a means of frank and open brain-
picking. For example, after his decision to have Lanny
Budd inherit one million dollars, with the stipulation
that he use it to achieve world peace, Sinclair wrote to
dozens of people—including diplomats, editors, politicians, scientists, scholars, and common laborers—asking
how they felt Lanny should spend the money. Sinclair
then used their responses as the basis for a discussion
among his fictional characters, with many of the people
consulted appearing in the novel (without disguise) to
advocate their ideas to Lanny.

It is clearly to Sinclair's advantage as a propagandist
to make his novels as "true" as possible, for if the reader
is persuaded that the events and persons and places
described correspond with the "facts" of history, he may
believe that the interpretation presented is equally accurate.

This method of writing fits in nicely with Sinclair's philosophy. Not only is literature to be an open attempt to influence the reader, but in order for the writer to feel confident in its validity, it is to be based on one's own research. The ideal would be to approach all novels in the way Sinclair wrote *The Jungle*. Sinclair first made a personal inspection of the area of investigation, then charged his story with the energy of personal experience. As he described the process in his *Autobiography*: "I wrote with tears and anguish, pouring into the pages all the pain that life had meant to me."

An older Sinclair, however, was physically unable to observe the events and conditions described in his novels. The Lanny Budd series, for example, attempted to discuss virtually everything that happened between the Versailles Treaty and the Korean War; and it was written during a period of time in which Sinclair rarely left his home. So, with regard to the events described in his later narratives, Sinclair depended heavily on published accounts and his personal correspondence with the makers of history to provide authenticity. With all the facts duly documented, then, Sinclair handled the important part of his story—the propaganda—through the use of clearly identified spokesmen.

Like his theory about the propagandistic purpose of literature, Sinclair's blatant use of a fictional mouthpiece is out of fashion. Influenced by writers such as Henry James, most of Sinclair's serious contemporaries tried to avoid dogmatic "intrusions" of the author into the worlds of their novels. But if literature is an attempt to place ideology before readers in an understandable way, an obvious spokesman becomes a convenient tool rather than a literary liability. In this way Sinclair hoped to produce "propaganda of vitality and importance"—propaganda defined by Sinclair as the spreading of democratic socialism.

Socialism, Sinclair's solution, is a problem for Americans. Sinclair's acceptance of this label, for millions of citizens, would be enough to consign him to a small (but dangerous) group of dissidents determined to subvert the American experiment in favor of something alien, totalitarian, and atheistic.

Far from a foreign ideology, Sinclair's concept of American socialism retained every significant aspect of an idealism often referred to as the American Dream. Sinclair's sermon was not advocation of dictatorship of an American proletariat by means of violent revolution. Rather than overthrowing traditional American values, he urged his audience to *return* to the vision that had, in his opinion, made America mankind's noblest attempt to achieve human brotherhood. Already in "My Cause" (1903) Sinclair had written:

It is my hope to do what one man can to make known to the men of our day the sacredness of this Republic, the blood and the tears and the agonies that sealed its foundation-stones. The future of the world lies in this Republic; and it faces perils to-day.

The Journal of Arthur Stirling, published the same year, has been identified by Sinclair as a spiritual autobiography. It contains passages suitable for American graduation ceremonies:

Chiefest of all I think of my country! Passionately, more than words can utter, I love this land of mine. If I tear my heart till it bleeds and pour out the tears of my spirit, it is for this consecration and this hope—it is for this land of Washington and Lincoln. There never was any land like it—there may never be any like it again; and Freedom watches from her mountains, trembling.

So when Sinclair attacked capitalism during the great depression in *The Way Out* (1933), he did so in terms of its *violation* of American values:

I maintain that there is no greater perversion in history than the identification of Americanism with capitalism. It is true that capitalism stands for liberty of a sort—the liberty to prey, to gamble, and to exploit. But these are very old kinds of liberty in the world, and America did not have to discover them. We are seeking to establish and to protect a new kind of liberty, to serve and to be at peace and to enjoy the fruits of one's own labour. Who shall say that such things are incompatible with the American spirit.

Sinclair called himself a socialist because he saw socialists as ideologists who embraced the implications of American liberalism more completely than do most Americans who call themselves liberals. And two more recent students of American socialism concur with his analysis:

Though it often seemed shaped by a foreign radicalism and some of its leaders spoke with accents that indicated a foreign birth, the American socialist movement owed more to its own country than to Europe. . . . Though decidedly socialist in its aim, the party taught democratic action, representative government, and a slow patient fight toward its socialist utopia. Its followers shunned revolutionary violence and talk of uprisings among the workers. Education was its key to success.[16]

There are certain characteristics common to Marxism and the American democratic tradition which therefore encourage similar tendencies in the arts. Thus, both Marxism and American democracy, in theory if not in practice, tend to emphasize the virtues of a classless society, although the one stresses economic equality in the ownership of the means of production, the other political equality combined with equality of economic opportunity.[17]

This is precisely what Sinclair was all about. In fact, if one lists the primary beliefs upon which Sinclair based the texts of his sermons over the years, one has a fairly comprehensive summary of what it means to be a "liberal" in the United States. His *Autobiography* stresses his continual belief in progress through the control of the social environment:

We manufacture crime wholesale, just as certainly and as definitely as we manufacture alcohol in a mash of grain. And just as we can stop getting alcohol by not mixing a mash, so we can stop crime by not permitting exploitation and economic inequality.

In *Letters to Judd* he endorses the "work" ethic: "If a fellow won't work, he has no right to anything—we agree to that, and we will shed no tears over shirkers and loafers." His campaign for the governorship of California was typical American politics. Sinclair contended that he would win because his program "was right, and the right has a way of prevailing." Simultaneously he advocated *realpolitik*: "Let us drop utopias from our program. No more ideal commonwealths, no more perfect solutions." Like most American liberals, he believed in the central planning of Franklin Roosevelt, who was "headed in the right direction, towards government control of business and industry." And like most American liberals, he also rejected "an un-American idea that we should trust our affairs to the management of people three thousand miles away from us."

Sinclair, I believe, personifies the relationship of socialism to America: "Thus in the art of the United States, as in other aspects of American life, any imported socialist content has usually been retained only when it reinforces already existing American tendencies."[18] Sinclair, as a liberal, accepted the goals associated with liberal ideas and the system provided to achieve those goals. Violent revolution, in his analysis, was unnecessary because of the freedom in America to advocate social solutions as a candidate for political office or as a writer of propaganda. Examination of the life and work of Upton Sinclair becomes an investigation of the liberal dilemma in America, for the man reflects the strengths and weaknesses of American liberalism throughout a long, impressive, and frustrating career.

2

The Preparation

Those who write of the art of poetry teach us that, if we would write what may be worth the reading, we ought always, before we begin, to form a regular plan and design of our piece; otherwise, we shall be in danger of incongruity. I am apt to think it is the same as to life. I have never fixed a regular design in life; by which means it has been a confused variety of different scenes. I am now entering upon a new one: let me, therefore, make some resolutions, and form some scheme of action, that, henceforth, I may live in all respects like a rational creature.

—Benjamin Franklin, *Autobiography.*

Since Upton Sinclair based his publications so extensively on personal concerns and experiences, it becomes pertinent to consider briefly the early part of his life, during which general attitudes took shape. In his first book of reminiscences, *American Outpost* (1932), Sinclair stressed the importance of having been born into a poor but aristocratic family. Remembering a childhood in Baltimore in terms of one-room lodgings and bedbugs, Sinclair developed an implacable hostility to alcohol. In his autobiographical portrayal of his father, presented in *Love's Pilgrimage* (1911) as well as in *American Outpost*, whiskey emerges, in Sinclair's words, as "the most conspicuous single fact in my boyhood." His father sold whiskey wholesale and earned enough money to support a family. But he could not keep himself from squandering his resources on liquor. He later sold clothing for men, "but he could never get away from drink, for the beginning of every deal was a 'treat,' and the close of it was another."

In 1931, Sinclair published *The Wet Parade*, a novel about prohibition. And in 1956 he returned to the subject of alcohol with *The Cup of Fury*, a book that included sociological arguments against drinking along with case histories of those who, in Sinclair's opinion, destroyed themselves with liquor—Ambrose Bierce, Theodore Dreiser, Jack London, Sinclair Lewis, Hart Crane, Dylan Thomas, George Sterling, O. Henry, Stephen Crane, Finley Peter Dunne, Eugene Debs, Isadora Duncan, William Seabrook, George Cram Cook, and Edna St. Vincent Millay.

As always, Sinclair's attempt was to adduce logical arguments for positions to which he was also emotionally committed. While he was aware that not everyone who drank alcohol was eventually ruined by the habit, as far as *The Cup of Fury* was concerned, total abstinence was the only logical position: "I cast my vote against social drinking. I will not keep a dog in my house that bites one of every five or nine people who stoop to pet it. Nor will I sanction alcohol because it dooms or harms 'just' one of every five, nine, or sixteen who drink it."

Whiskey was connected to Sinclair's conception of aristocracy as well as to his experience of poverty, since his father was "the youngest son of Captain Arthur Sinclair" and "all Southern gentlemen 'drank.'" In *American Outpost*, Sinclair, the enemy of class distinctions, went to great length to emphasize his aristocratic pedigree in order to establish himself as a critic from within. His great-grandfather, Arthur Sinclair, was a Commodore in the U. S. Navy who fought on the Great Lakes during the War of 1812. His grandfather, also a naval officer, was drowned while attempting to bring supplies to the Confederacy. His mother's father, John S. Harden, was a high official of the Western Maryland Railroad. His maternal grandmother's ancestry could be traced back to "several castles in Ireland." And much of his early childhood was spent in the home of his mother's sister, who "married John R. Bland, a descendant of John Randolph, the Virginia statesman."

So personal experience with both poverty and wealth became Sinclair's basis for his class analysis of American society. In his *Autobiography* he announced:

Readers of my novels know that I have one favorite theme, the contrast between the social classes; there are characters from both worlds, the rich and the poor, and the plots are contrived to carry you from one to the other. The explanation is that as far back as I can remember, my life was a series of Cinderella transformations; one night I would be sleeping on a vermin-ridden sofa in a lodging-house, and the next night under silken coverlets in a fashionable home.

Rejection of his father's behavior was cited by Sinclair as the basic reason for his close identification with his mother, his consequent respect for women, and his later championing of women's suffrage. And his early interest in literature was based on equally personal motivation:

The sordid surroundings in which I was forced to live as a child made me a dreamer. I took to literature, because that was the earliest refuge.
While arguments between my father and my mother were going on, I was with Gulliver in Lilliput, or on the way to the Celestial City with Christian, or in the shop with the little tailor who killed "seven at one blow."

In the winter of 1888, the Sinclair family moved to New York City, and although Upton was ten years old before he entered the public schools, he received significant education in the city streets. As they moved from apartment to apartment, each "in turn was home, each neighborhood full of wonder and excitement. Second Avenue was especially thrilling, because the 'gangs' came out from Avenue A and Avenue B, like Sioux or Pawnees in war paint, and well-dressed little boys had to fly for their lives."

Given a late start in formal education, Sinclair managed to pass through the eight elementary grades within two years. He was ready, at twelve years of age, for the College of the City of New York, "in reality only a high school." The "college," however, had a minimal matriculation age of fourteen years, so Upton returned for further schooling from the "East Side toughs" of Twenty-third Street. In 1892, five days before his fourteenth birthday, he became a subfreshman at the college, and he soon made his first move in the direction of professional writing.

Imitating a classmate who had gotten a story published, Sinclair turned one of his pet birds into a messen-
ger in a story about an innocent black youth accused of
arson. *Argosy* bought it for twenty-five dollars and thus
convinced Sinclair that he could earn a living by writing.
Stranded by a drinking father, he shared expenses with
his mother, spending $4.25 per week for board and room,
plus an additional quarter "for a clean collar and other
luxuries."

Sinclair discovered that the going rate for jokes was
one dollar each, and contributions such as the following
became what he, himself, later called an obsession:

Old Lady—You look as if you never washed, sir.
Weary Will—Yes, Ma'am; I prefer godliness.[1]

Whatever the quality of the humor, Sinclair's method of
covering the market anticipated the systematic way in
which he would approach his later writing. In his *Autobiography* he writes:

I wrote out my jokes on slips of paper, with a number in
the corner, and sent them in batches of ten to the different
editors; when the pack came back with one missing, I had
earned a dollar. I had a bookkeeping system, showing where
each batch had been sent; jokes number 321 to 330 had been
sent to *Life, Judge,* and *Puck,* and were now at the *Evening
Journal.*

After five years Sinclair graduated, in the middle of
his class, and he moved from jokes and stories to larger
units of writing as he advanced from City College to
Columbia University to study literature and philosophy.
Quantitatively, his writing career while a graduate student there is simply astounding.

For a New York publisher, Street and Smith, Sinclair began to churn out the Mark Mallory stories, a

series of nickel novels, written under the pen names of Lieutenant Frederick Garrison, U. S. Army, and Ensign Clarke Fitch, U. S. Navy. Sinclair hired two stenographers to take dictation for three hours every afternoon. While he was attending classes in the morning, these stenographers would type the previous day's dictation, giving Sinclair a written copy for evening revisions.

The result of this was "a novelette of close to thirty thousand words every week," for which he received forty dollars. Later he increased his earnings to seventy dollars per week by raising his daily word total to eight thousand words and working on Sundays. According to Floyd Dell, "At the age of twenty, he was turning out more than two million words a year."[2] In his *Autobiography*, Sinclair figured that by the time he had left graduate school at the turn of the century he "had published an output equal in volume to the works of Walter Scott."

Again giving a very personal explanation for his behavior, Sinclair has concluded that his output was based on sexual repression. Subject to what he called "storms of craving," Sinclair was determined to preserve his chastity until marriage, thus holding onto his ideal "dream of a noble and beautiful love." So it was, perhaps, an unusual student who had to leave his study of Renaissance art because the nakedness encountered was too overwhelming. But Sinclair considered his behavior a useful channeling of energy: "I learned to work fourteen hours a day at study and creative effort because it was only by being thus occupied that the craving for woman could be kept out of my soul," he told us in his *Autobiography*.

Typically, Sinclair could identify qualities within himself and manipulate them into becoming desirable forces. If one approves the goals attained, the evaluation emerging will be that of a disciplined, idealistic reformer. If not, Sinclair would offer an alternate diagnosis "as an advanced case of delusion of grandeur, messianic complex, paranoia, narcissism, and so to the end. . . ."

Sinclair went to the university determined to develop his mind into a tool that could correct the wretched condition of the world he saw around him. Calling this endeavor "going in for the genius business," he was in no way interested in a degree to be used as a meal ticket. Thus he paid the $150 tuition fee required of Columbia University students for a master's degree, intentionally failed to complete his courses, and consequently was able to attend lectures for four years at no extra cost.

But as his later books, *The Goose-step* and *The Goslings*, were to make abundantly clear, Sinclair was less than satisfied with American educational institutions. Most of the professors, he felt, were dull plodders "who dealt with the bones and dust of inspirations." Famous educators such as Nicholas Murray Butler and Brander Matthews served as negative models for Sinclair, who was determined not to teach like them.

He was equally sure, however, that any twentieth-century genius should have an adequate familiarity with the thoughts of great minds of the past. So in his "usual one-track fashion," he "concentrated on German literature and for a year or so read nothing else." Having ingested the essential works of Schiller, Heine, Lessing, Herder, Wagner, Kant, and countless lesser Germans, he decided to master French and Italian literature in the original. His book of literary criticism, *Mammonart*, shows that after these student years of voracious reading, Sinclair felt himself qualified to evaluate the work of practically every Western writer of significance between Homer and Jack London.

Sinclair's main complaint about his educational experience in a major university was that it failed to inform him about socialism. It was not until 1902 that he discovered that he would have allies in the project of world correction:

It was like the falling down of prison walls about my mind; the most amazing discovery, after all these years—that I did not have to carry the whole burden of humanity's future upon my two frail shoulders! There were actually others who understood. . . . The principal fact which the Socialists had to teach me, was the fact that they existed.

So Sinclair's view of himself when he stopped formal study in 1900 was that of a naive youth who did not yet have any real insights into the workings of the world, but who had read widely enough to place those insights into context when they came, and who had developed a rigorous self-discipline that would enable him to work tirelessly in the correct direction once it was discovered.

First, however, Sinclair was to go through an apprenticeship of the emotions in order to balance the training his mind had been given. Emotion and reason were always closely related for Sinclair. The man who directed his sexual energy toward "rational" goals felt that "marriage can be studied as a science, and practiced as an art." Not all of his art work was, in his own opinion, successful. He presented his painful relationship with Meta Fuller, whom he married in 1900, to his readers with typical Sinclarian honesty.

To discuss the failure of his first marriage, Sinclair went to classical pastoral poetry (filtered through Milton's "L'Allegro") to find names suitable for suggesting the idyllic companionship anticipated by the two young lovers. Calling himself Thyrsis and his wife Corydon, in *Love's Pilgrimage* and in his autobiographies he allows us to look at this part of his life through these characters. Their marriage, he wrote, was wrong from the start, based on almost complete ignorance of male/female relationships. Thyrsis, although penniless, was certain that with *Springtime and Harvest* (Sinclair's first serious book) he had written The Great American Novel. So against the wishes of both families the two lovers were wed. But no publishers wanted the book, a romantic tale of a beautiful woman who marries a cripple for his money—a work that embarrassed Sinclair later since it was not grounded in personal experience or socialist theory.

Supporting himself and his wife by writing the now despised potboilers, Sinclair managed to save enough money to get *Springtime and Harvest* published at his own expense in January of 1901. He sent copies to the New York newspapers, but managed to sell only two copies of the novel to people who did not know him personally. Meta became pregnant, and the Sinclairs were investigating abortion possibilities when an editor's unexpected praise of the book led to an acceptance by Funk and Wagnalls, who reissued it as *King Midas*.

But a new title was no touch of gold for the struggling couple. So in the spring of 1902 they hoped to increase inspiration and decrease costs by moving into a small tent located on a remote island in Lake Erie. With his pregnant wife in the hammock beside him, Sinclair wrote *Prince Hagen*, "the story of a Nibelung, grandson of the dwarf Alberich, who brings his golden treasures up to Wall Street and Fifth Avenue, and proves the identity between our Christian civilization and his own dark realm."

Back in New York City for the winter, Sinclair continued his unsuccessful efforts to interest publishers in his serious work. Meta returned to the home of her parents, but the young husband joined her for the birth of their son, David, in December. They separated again the next summer, with Upton returning to the island retreat to write *The Journal of Arthur Stirling* and Meta going with her family to the Catskills.

With his literary ambitions continually frustrated, the usually honest Sinclair decided to try what he considered to be a harmless hoax. To create a sensational effect, he published *The Journal of Arthur Stirling* as the autobiographical work of a bitter young poet who had just committed suicide. A friend inserted accounts of the "death" into New York papers, and D. Appleton and Company became interested in the publication of the "diary." Sinclair explained his hoax to the literary adviser of the company, Ripley Hitchcock. He did not object, and the book was published in February of 1903, creating "a tremendous furore." One reviewer, but not many readers, found the book "at once an authoritative document, a heart-searching appeal, and a tragic entertainment."[3]

Sinclair's trick did not make him wealthy, and his financial plight made him receptive to the message he was beginning to encounter in socialist publications. He wrote to George D. Herron, the author of one such pamphlet, and a developing friendship eventually resulted in Herron agreeing to give Sinclair several hundred dollars plus a monthly subsidy of thirty dollars to finance the next writing project—a trilogy about the Civil War to be entitled *The American*.

With minimal financial support at last, the Sinclair family was reunited. The old summer tent was placed on a wooden platform, located in some woods outside Princeton, New Jersey, where Sinclair had access to the excellent Civil War holdings of the university library.

Only the first volume was ever written. The first of

Sinclair's realistic novels, *Manassas* (1904) included battle scenes that Floyd Dell considered superior to those in *The Red Badge of Courage*. And most of the issues —the economic feasibility of slavery, the constitutional right of secession—are argued clearly by Sinclair's characters. But contemporary readers, used to war novels like *The Naked and the Dead* and *Catch-22*, will probably find the language and adventures of Allan Montague too genteel to be convincing.

While writing *Manassas*, Sinclair became increasingly committed to socialism. He began regular reading of the *Appeal to Reason*, a socialist weekly published in Kansas, and he decided that his interest in chattel slavery should be directed toward a consideration of his contemporary American wage slaves. So he stopped work on the trilogy, accepted a $500 cash advance (for serial rights) from the *Appeal to Reason*, and went to Chicago in October of 1904 to gather data. He returned to Princeton, moved to a farmhouse, and settled down on Christmas Day to three months of the intensive writing that was to culminate in the most sensational book of his career.

3

The Muckraker

Give me your tired, your poor,
Your huddled masses yearning to breathe free
The wretched refuse of your teeming shore.
Send these, the homeless, tempest-tost to me,
I lift my lamp beside the golden door.

—Emma Lazarus

When the Statue of Liberty was dedicated in 1886, the poetic sentiments carved on its pedestal had already achieved the status of national mystique. But the response to the invitation went beyond the imaginations of the Founding Fathers who had identified America as a land offering liberty and justice for all. During the first ten years of this century, 8,795,386 immigrants entered the United States. Although 8,136,016 of the people came from Europe, less than a half million were from Great Britain, whereas the number included more than two million Italians and another two million from Austria and Hungary. Certainly the Pilgrims, despite seeing themselves as models to be emulated, would never have predicted that within a single decade 1,597,306 Russians would follow their example in choosing this New World.[1]

Since he wanted to give a current report on the state of the American experiment, Sinclair's creation of a Lithuanian immigrant family was quite appropriate. For significant Russian immigration (including Lithuanians) was a recent phenomenon. In 1880 only five thousand Russians emigrated to the United States. But this number increased steadily until 1907, one year after *The Jungle* was published, when more than a quarter of a million Russians bet their lives that America was their promised land.[2]

If these were new sorts of immigrants, they were coming for traditional economic and religious reasons. And Sinclair, who never separated his economic condition from his spiritual or psychological state, was increasingly convinced that without socialism America could offer these new believers in the American Dream only a nightmarish existence. In 1905, while working on *The Jungle*, he took time to organize the Intercollegiate Socialist Society. Never again—if people like Sinclair, Jack London, Harry Laidler, and Norman Thomas could help it

30

—would it be possible for someone to graduate from a university without being aware of the socialist solution. But it was his novel that called the attention of the world to Upton Sinclair. For his portrayal of Lithuanian peasants who come to America vividly suggests that our melting pot is less appetizing than the terms offered on our Statue of Liberty.

Jurgis Rudkis and Ona Lukoszaite, whose marriage in America constitutes the first chapter of *The Jungle,* had met in Brelovicz one and a half years earlier. It was true love at first sight, and "without ever having spoken a word to her, with no more than the exchange of half a dozen smiles, he found himself, purple in the face with embarrassment and terror, asking her parents to sell her to him for his wife." But Ona's father was rich and Jurgis was poor; so his application was denied. Then financial disaster struck the Lukoszaite family with the death of the father. Jurgis returned to find that "the prize was within his reach."

At the advice of Jonas, the brother of Ona's step-mother, they decide to go to America, "a place of which lovers and young people dreamed," a land where "rich or poor, a man was free." So the twelve Lithuanians—Jurgis and Ona, his father, her stepmother (and six children), Uncle Jonas, Cousin Marija—come to America, believing the advertisements about opportunities for anyone willing to work.

Throughout the first part of the book, Jurgis's response to increasing trouble is the one endorsed by Benjamin Franklin. When he finds that many of his wedding guests, especially the young ones, are abusing a time-honored custom by not contributing toward the costs of the affair he says, "I will work harder." When Ona panics at his suggestion that she take a day's honey-moon away from work "he answers her again: 'Leave it to me; leave it to me. I will earn more money—I will work harder'."

The immigrants, as Sinclair describes them, are faced with the difficult task of retaining desirable aspects of an old way of life—their music, their religion, their concept of family—within a new setting that affords, supposedly, the chance to succeed economically via personal efforts. According to scholars such as Oscar Handlin, this effort was doomed to fail from the time they got on board the boat in Europe: "The qualities that were desirable in the good peasant were not those conducive to success in the transition. Neighborliness, obedience, respect, and status were valueless among the masses that struggled for space on the way."[3]

Not only do old ways fall victim to new conditions in Sinclair's novel, but the promise of equal economic opportunity for which these old values were sacrificed turns out to be fraudulent. Again Handlin supports Sinclair's earlier analysis: "It was characteristic that, about then [1900], for every hundred dollars earned by native wage earners, the Italian-born earned eighty-four, the Hungarians sixty-eight, and the other Europeans fifty-four."[4]

Sinclair's title indicates that American society, in his analysis, had returned to the law of the jungle, where might makes right in a brutal survival of the fittest. But Sinclair was in no way one of those theorists who sought to apply the biological insights of Darwin to the realm of social relationships. John Higham has observed that "in their eagerness to convert social values into biological facts, Darwinian optimists unblinkingly read 'the fittest' to mean 'the best.' "[5]

Sinclair directly opposed this. Rather than praising competition as a healthy and natural process—with cream always rising to the top—Sinclair accepted the contradictory value of cooperation. Competition, the socially inadequate law of the jungle, turns men into brutes in his novel:

Every day the police net would drag hundreds of them off the streets, and in the Detention Hospital you might see them, herded together in a miniature inferno, with hideous, beastly faces, bloated and leprous with disease, laughing, shouting, screaming in all stages of drunkenness, barking like dogs, gibbering like apes, raving and tearing themselves in delirium.

Those who survived the dehumanizing competition inherent in capitalism were likely to be the least fit morally. Later, in *The Goslings*, Sinclair would refer to Yale's professor of political economy, William Graham Sumner (a leading Social Darwinist), as "a prime minister in the empire of plutocratic education." And what Sumner called an objective analysis of the way society had to operate was called by Sinclair the deification of the most brutish sort of selfishness, "covered by the mantle of science." In short, the classic Social Darwinist statement of John D. Rockefeller represents quite precisely those ideas that Sinclair felt were antithetical to the American Dream:

The growth of a large business is merely a survival of the fittest. . . . The American Beauty rose can be produced in the splendor and fragrance which bring cheer to its beholder only by sacrificing the early buds which grow up around it. This is not an evil tendency in business. It is merely the working-out of a law of nature and a law of God.[6]

In Sinclair's book, his version of reality, Jurgis cannot succeed financially without exchanging his high morality and willingness to work for a cynical acceptance of the need to lie, cheat, steal, and exploit others. He gets his first job in Packingtown—the name used to refer to the stockyards district of Chicago—with ease, because he stands out as a fresh young stalwart among the rest of the applicants. Having completed a tour of his new environment, he is prepared to face his first day's work with energetic enthusiasm: "He had dressed hogs himself in the forest of Lithuania; but he had never expected to live to see one hog dressed by several hundred men. It was like a wonderful poem to him, and he took it all in guilelessly."

With the whole clan contributing, Jurgis is able to put together enough money for the down payment on a home—another opportunity they would not have had in feudal Europe. But the contract is rigged so that if they ever miss a payment they will lose the house. Jurgis eventually understands this, and decides to work harder so that such a disaster will not occur. He makes the same response when he discovers that his monthly payments do not include the annual interest fee.

After one summer of work by the whole family, enough money is accumulated "for Jurgis and Ona to be married according to home traditions of decency." But the first winter brings the first death. Jurgis's father contracts a fatal disease, probably tuberculosis, from working in a filthy cellar. Stanislovas, Ona's fourteen-year-old stepbrother, is a psychological victim of the same winter. Although he continued to work at filling lard cans for five cents per hour, he "conceived a terror of the cold that was almost a mania" as a result of having seen his partner's frozen ears drop off when they were rubbed too vigorously.

The financial contribution of Marija, who earned even more than Jurgis by painting cans, stops without warning when the canning factory closes for the winter. For Jurgis, too, winter is a slack season. Although he is expected to be available at the "killing beds" all day, he is paid only for those hours when he actually works; this system often reduces his income to about thirty-five cents per day. In order to make the twelve-dollar monthly house payment, meet the extra expenses of coal and winter clothing, and feed the clan, Jurgis once again decides he will simply have to work harder.

Spring arrives, and so does a son, little Antanas. Ona develops "womb trouble" from going back to work too quickly. But "the great majority of the women who worked in Packingtown suffered in the same way, and from the same cause, so it was not deemed a thing to see the doctor about." Summer provides a chance to build up financial and physical reserves for the second Chicago winter.

The first snowstorm hits just before Christmas, making it impossible for the weakened Ona to walk to the spot on the line where she sewed hams all day. But "the soul of Jurgis rose up within him like a sleeping lion." Starting out before dawn, he carries Ona through snowdrifts that come up to his armpits, repeating the performance around eleven o'clock every night.

But chance events can confound even the most physically fit. Upon occasion a steer would break loose on the killing beds, running amuck among workers who scramble over bloody floors to get behind pillars so that when "the floor boss would come rushing up with a rifle and begin blazing away" they could be counted among the survivors. During one such adventure Jurgis sprains his ankle and is unable to stand on his feet for two weeks. To make matters worse, Jonas, the brother of Ona's stepmother, decides that personal interests weigh more than family loyalty; he disappears, reducing the total income of the household while house payments remain constant.

Jurgis goes back to work before his ankle is healed,

but he cannot function, so he loses his job. Now the family must try harder; the two younger brothers of Stanislovas, aged eleven and ten, become part of America's work force by selling newspapers. During this time one of the youngest children dies, probably from eating "tubercular pork that was condemned as unfit for export," but legal fare for Europeans who had come to America.

After two months Jurgis is able to walk again, but since he is no longer a prime physical specimen the only place in Packingtown where he can get a job is the fertilizer plant.

To this part of the yards came all the "tankage," and the waste products of all sorts; here they dried out the bones— and in suffocating cellars, where the daylight never came, you might see men and women and children bending over whirling machines and sawing bits of bone into all sorts of shapes, breathing their lungs full of the fine dust, and doomed to die, every one of them, within a certain definite time.

Jurgis spends his third American summer there, and while he is able to make all of the house payments on time, his home falls apart. He and Ona have little to talk about, and they are generally too weary to care about each other. But remnants of old values remain. Thus when Jurgis discovers the following winter that Ona has slept with her boss in order to retain her job, he attacks the man viciously, gets himself thrown in jail for one month, and returns to find that the house is repainted—sold as new to brand-new victims.

He finally finds his family, lodged in the cheapest garret of a boardinghouse, and enters to hear the screams of Ona dying in childbirth—an eighteen-year-old worn-out woman. He discovers that because of his attack on Ona's boss he is blacklisted, unable to work anywhere in Packingtown. This is almost overwhelming, but Jurgis's hopes are raised again when he finds relatively desirable work at the Harvester plant. The job lasts nine dáys; then the works are closed until further notice. He moves to a steel mill, works four days, and burns his hand so severely that he is laid off for more than a week. Then little Antanas drowns in the mud of Chicago's streets, and Jurgis becomes a cynic.

All this time Jurgis had been relatively successful in withstanding the temptation to escape his environment in the way chosen by most of the workers—alcohol. Now, rather than turning to drink, he decides to escape altogether. Jurgis walks out on the rest of Ona's relatives and becomes a hobo. When a farmer refuses to give him some food, he tears up one hundred young peach trees by the roots, thus demonstrating that he has adapted to America.

Jurgis wanders around the countryside for a summer, learning much about wine and women, and then returns to Chicago in the winter to help dig freight tunnels. A fight with a bartender leads to a second short jail term. But this time he makes friends with a professional thief who introduces Jurgis to the criminal underworld. Graduating from theft to political illegalities, Jurgis rises quite rapidly. He becomes a "foreman," placed back on the killing beds to insure the election of selected politicians every voting day.

Then a remnant of integrity from his past arises to plague him again. He meets Ona's old boss by chance and instinctively repeats his attack. His political friends are able to help him avoid a prison sentence, but he is now of little use to them and he must return to the life of a Chicago bum—stealing cabbages from grocers, drinking cheap beer for the sake of shelter, begging for funds to finance a night in a flophouse.

While begging, he discovers the address of Cousin Marija, who has become a prostitute. He visits her, hoping for some help, and learns that Stanislovas has been killed and eaten by rats after having been locked into his factory overnight by mistake.

Back on the street, Jurgis has no particular place to go, so in order to stay warm he enters a building in which a political rally is being held. He listens to a socialist speaker who correctly predicts that the "scales will fall from his eyes, the shackles will be torn from his limbs—he will leap up with a cry of thankfulness, he will stride forth a free man at last!"

Within a week of his conversion Jurgis finds a job at a small hotel run by a socialist. He begins to work at his new life with his old diligence. He reads much socialist literature and soon has enough money to support Ona's relatives again. (Marija, however, has become a dope addict, and "chooses" to remain a prostitute.) By the end of the novel Jurgis has become a thoroughly convinced socialist, part of the social movement that he and Sinclair expected to turn Chicago into a place fit for Americans.

Sinclair's novel is remembered, and rightly so, for its graphic descriptions of working conditions in Packingtown. But only about half of the book is concerned with the meat-packing industry, and even this half is used as a vehicle for Sinclair's larger message. What had happened to the spirit of America? What devil had tempted the American mind to substitute cash for value, thus allowing this intended Garden of Eden to go to seed—nourished by the heat of industrialization into a jungle of greed and grease and despair?

For Sinclair, bringing democracy to industry represented an answer to both economic and spiritual questions. He was not the first American to come to this conclusion. Earlier socialists, such as Edward Bellamy, had seen history as a working out of the gradual advance of the democratic principle. The Protestant Reformation had acknowledged all men as equal in status before God. The American and French Revolutions had introduced political equality. Now it was necessary to add economic equality in order to allow men their natural right to a humane and fulfilling existence.

Sinclair (who believed this) was a muckraker determined to expose the inhumanity of capitalism so that Americans could opt for an economic system more closely aligned with their accepted ideals. Not all muckrakers had such extensive ideological motivations. According to Richard Hofstadter, most

outstanding figures of the muckrake era were simply writers or reporters working on commission and eager to do well what was asked of them. A few, among them Upton Sinclair and Gustavus Myers, were animated by a deep-going dislike of the capitalist order, but most of them were hired into muckraking or directed toward it on the initiative of sales-conscious editors or publishers.[7]

As Hofstadter demonstrates, "what was new in muckraking in the Progressive era was neither its ideas nor its existence, but its reach—its nationwide character and its capacity to draw nationwide attention. . . ."[8] So there was an element of fad in the success of Sinclair's novel. But since his goal was to upset an irrational economic system, he was scarcely satisfied by causing a nation to regurgitate. In *Cosmopolitan Magazine* (October 1906) Sinclair wrote:

Perhaps you will be surprised to be told that I failed in my purpose, when you know of all the uproar that "The Jungle" has been creating. But then that uproar is all accidental and was due to an entirely different cause. I wished to frighten the country by a picture of what its industrial masters were doing to their victims; entirely by chance I had stumbled on another discovery—what they were doing to the meat-supply of the civilized world. In other words, I aimed at the public's heart, and by accident I hit it in the stomach.

Two passages will suffice to show why the blow to the stomach was a direct hit:

There were the wool pluckers, whose hands went to pieces even sooner than the hands of the pickle men; for the pelts of the sheep had to be painted with acid to loosen the wool, and then the pluckers had to pull out this wool with their bare hands, till the acid had eaten their fingers off. . . . As for the other men, who worked in tank rooms full of steam, and in some of which there were open vats near the level of the floor, their peculiar trouble was that they fell into the vats; and when they were fished out, there was never enough of them left to be worth exhibiting—sometimes they would be overlooked for days, till all but the bones of them had gone out to the world as Durham's Pure Leaf Lard!

There would be meat that had tumbled out on the floor, in the dirt and sawdust, where the workers had tramped and spit uncounted billions of consumption germs. There would be meat stored in great piles in rooms; and the water from leaky roofs would drip over it, and thousands of rats would race about on it. It was too dark in these storage places to see well, but a man could run his hand over these piles of meat and sweep up handfuls of the dried dung of rats. These rats were nuisances, and the packers would put poisoned bread out for them, they would die, and then rats, bread, and meat would go into the hoppers together. This is no fairy story and no joke. . . .

To treat it fairly then, *The Jungle* must be considered from two points of view. Historically, it provided the impetus for useful legislation. Few writers accomplish this, and it should be remembered that Sinclair's goal was to affect the lives of his readers. For an understanding of why Sinclair considered it a failure, however, the novel must be evaluated in terms of his larger purpose—converting a populace to democratic socialism. But first let us outline the impact of the successful social document.

Sinclair had trouble getting his dramatic statement onto center stage. Although it had been serialized by the *Appeal to Reason*, Sinclair wanted to reach an audience not already committed to socialism. Five publishers rejected it because, says Sinclair in his *Autobiography*, "nothing so horrible had ever been published in America —at least not by a respectable concern." The eventual publishers—Doubleday, Page & Co.—felt obliged to send their own lawyer, Thomas H. McKee, to investigate the industry before they risked publication. McKee's report supported Sinclair, and the book was published in February of 1906.

The Jungle immediately became the sensation of the day. The meat-packing scandal was front-page newspaper material for weeks, with Sinclair's name constantly attached. Supporting Hofstadter's contention that the only thing new about muckrakers was their ability to get attention, after Sinclair's exposé had aroused the nation and President Roosevelt, General Nelson Miller lamented the fact that outrage had come seven years too late for many Americans. He estimated that three thousand soldiers had died of "embalmed" beef during the Spanish-American War. But although he had collected the evidence and was prepared to produce two thousand witnesses, he could not find anyone in Congress who wished to open this particular can of worms.[9]

Within a month the *Saturday Evening Post* pub-

lished articles, signed by J. Ogden Armour, which
defended the meat industry. The major packers, in
Armour's view, were being falsely maligned. Actually,
their impact upon America was benevolent, producing
fresh and inexpensive meat as well as important byprod-
ucts used for medical research and glue. With respect to
the cleanliness of America's meat, the defense was without qualification:

In Armour & Co.'s business *not one atom of any condemned
animal or carcass finds its way, directly or indirectly, from
any source, into any food product or food ingredient.*

Every meat animal and every carcass slaughtered in the
Union Stockyards, or in the stock yards at any of the
markets of the United States, is carefully inspected by the
United States Government.

Readers were invited to believe that Government inspection "is the wall that stands between the meat-eating
public and the sale of diseased meat."[10]

Sinclair responded with a public statement in which
he listed specific charges against Armour, openly inviting
a libel suit so that the issues could be decided in a court
of law.[11] And in May, *Everybody's* published "The
Condemned Meat Industry," in which Sinclair described
at length the attempt to bribe Thomas F. Dolan, a
former superintendent at Armour's & Co., who had
signed an affidavit supporting Sinclair's claims. (Dolan
accepted $5000 from Armour, and then published
accounts of the bribe; let the buyer beware.) To
Armour's contention that all meat was inspected, Sinclair added the information that this was to the benefit
of foreign consumers only. Meat condemned by the federal officials could not be sold *abroad*.

Theodore Roosevelt, who was opposed to muck-

rakers in general,* had eaten the army's canned meat in
Cuba, so he was prepared to believe the worst. He
invited Sinclair to Washington to discuss the issue, and
he agreed to send Charles P. Neill (Labor Commis-
sioner) and James B. Reynolds (Assistant Secretary of
the Treasury) to Chicago to investigate.

The meat industry continued to maintain its asser-
tions of purity. According to Congressman Wharton,
representative of the meat-packing district in Chicago:

The thing is all started from that book, and I know of my
own knowledge that there is no foundation of fact in it. . . .
I live in the packing district of Chicago. I know all about
it. I know those packing houses as well as I know the cor-
ridors of the capitol. . . . Why, there is not a kitchen of a
rich man in this city, or any other, that is any cleaner, if it
is as clean, as those places.

Of course, you know the sort of men many of the
laborers in the packing houses are—foreigners of a low
grade of intelligence—and you know how impossible it is
to control every individual. If those men happen to want to
spit, they are likely to spit, but it doesn't go on the meat.
That is nonsense. . . . 12

But the report of the federal investigators, kept
secret at first (to Sinclair's public dismay), convinced
President Roosevelt that present conditions were revolt-
ing. So he asked for a new law providing federal inspection for meat intended for domestic consumption. On
26 May 1906, the Senate passage of the Meat Inspection
Bill was headlined in the New York *Times* as a "Direct
Consequence of the Disclosures Made in Upton Sinclair's

* Roosevelt coined the term, intending it as a hostile label—
drawn from the Man with the Muckrake in Bunyan's *Pilgrim's
Progress* who devotes his time to the consideration of filth.

Novel." An amended House of Representatives version
and the final compromise law were both passed in June
of that year.

So Sinclair's success with *The Jungle*, on these
terms, was significant. But it was not what he had in
mind. It should be remembered that Sinclair wanted his
writing to be very personal. *The Jungle*, in his opinion,
was unlike the work of his contemporary producers of
realistic literature because, as he wrote in *Cosmopolitan
Magazine*, it was "written from the inside . . . the result
of an attempt to combine the best of two widely different schools; to put the content of Shelley into the form
of Zola." And Sinclair, personally, cared little about
meat, since he rarely ate it.

But he did care deeply about what the meat industry typified and represented—the apparent failure on the
part of American society to live up to established American ideals. The fact that his reading public responded
to what he described as a symptom indicates his failure
to communicate the more important concern about the
basic illness.

Several explanations are supportable. Literature
becomes impressive and memorable as it reduces
abstract concepts to concrete examples. It is easier to
remember that children's fingers, cows' fetuses, and rat
dung, are the unlisted ingredients in deviled ham than
that workers are oppressed, by definition, in a capitalist
economy. Few readers, no matter how sympathetic, have
found Sinclair's later chapters on socialist solutions to
be as gripping as his preceding presentation of free
enterprise at work. Through Jurgis, the reader learns
about the advantages and imminence of socialism. But
the speeches are tacked onto a plot that stops moving
when Jurgis sits down to listen.

Sinclair, agreeing that the conclusion is weak, posits

another explanation—one that fits in perfectly with his analysis of the interwining of economic and spiritual concerns. He was too *poor* to turn his socialistic sermons into a more effective ending of *The Jungle*. In his *Autobiography* he writes: "The last chapters were not up to standard, because both my health and my money were gone, and a second trip to Chicago, which I had hoped to make, was out of the question."

In 1909 Sinclair again had reason to comment on the pernicious effect of money upon his career:

Suffice it to say that never have I been able to write a single thing as I would have liked to write it, because of money. Either I was dead broke and had to rush it; or I knew that if I had my way, the public would not read it and the publishers would not accept it. Think of my having to ruin *The Jungle* with an ending so pitifully inadequate, because we were actually without money for food.[13]

But even if philosophic solutions are harder to dramatize than scandalous situations, and even if Sinclair's efforts to make those solutions come to literary life were impeded by financial concerns, the public's positive response to Sinclair's described symptom (meat-packing conditions) while ignoring his deeper diagnosis (capitalistic greed), probably has more to do with audience than with author. If the story is read as exposing a scandal, a law can be passed, inspectors can be appointed to enforce that law, and we the people can receive a sense of continuing progress. This is far more palatable than reading the story as an indictment of one's entire way of life. To miss the basic point of any Sinclair writing requires strong motivation on the part of the reader. To look at what Sinclair was trying to teach is to discover what Americans were determined not to learn about themselves.

Beneath the rhetoric of a new society based on equality and brotherhood, America had built its experiment on tried and tested foundations of competition and greed. As indicated above, Jurgis personifies the willingness to accept individual responsibility for his own situation. He sets out across an ocean to solve his own problems through his own honest efforts; he wants to work. But by the turn of the century this point of view had become a demonstration of naiveté rather than of healthy optimism. Jurgis's co-laborers had already discovered that the game was rigged to allow only a few winners. So their response is the complete negation of the American Dream; they hate to work.

They hated the bosses and they hated the owners; they hated the whole place, the whole neighborhood—even the whole city, with an all-inclusive hatred, bitter and fierce. Women and little children would fall to cursing about it; it was rotten, rotten as hell—everything was rotten.

For Sinclair, this undesirable result was built into the very theory of competitive capitalism:

Here was Durham's, for instance, owned by a man who was trying to make as much money out of it as he could, and did not care in the least how he did it, and underneath him, ranged in ranks and grades like an army, were managers and superintendents and foremen, each one driving the man next below him and trying to squeeze out of him as much work as possible.

Men are not essentially evil, but within capitalism immoral behavior is systematically rewarded. Continuing his authorial comment in *The Jungle*, Sinclair contended:

You could lay that down for a rule—if you met a man who was rising in Packingtown, you met a knave. . . . The man who told tales and spied upon his fellows would rise; but

the man who minded his own business and did his work—
why, they would "speed him up" till they had worn him out,
and then they would throw him into the gutter.

Consequently, good men turn vicious in order to
survive. Jurgis, who tries desperately to retain traditional
values, yields to the stronger forces of inhumanity at
the death of his son, "tearing up all the flowers from the
garden of his soul, and setting his heel upon them." But
Jurgis's creator retains those ideals, and he is in charge
of the direction of the book. In his expression of very
traditional American optimism, Sinclair believes that
democracy will come to American industry because right
eventually triumphs:

Those who lost in the struggle were generally exterminated;
but now and then they had been known to save themselves
by combination—which was a new and higher kind of
strength. It was so that the gregarious animals had overcome
the predaceous; it was so, in human history, that the people had mastered the kings. The workers were simply the
citizens of industry, and the Socialist movement was the
expression of their will to survive.

Sinclair's happy ending, the conversion of Jurgis to
a rational method of social organization, is made complete and personal via a charge of emotional energy:

The voice of Labor, despised and outraged; a mighty giant,
lying prostrate—mountainous, colossal, but blinded, bound,
and ignorant of his strength. And now a dream of resistance
haunts him, hope battling with fear; until suddenly he stirs,
and a fetter snaps—and a thrill shoots through him, to the
farthest ends of his huge body, and in a flash the dream becomes an act! . . . He springs to his feet, he shouts in his
new-born exultation—

Nothing could be more traditionally American than
the belief that this happy ending was inevitable since

God was counted on the good side of the struggle. Socialism, for Sinclair, "was the new religion of humanity—or you might say it was the fulfillment of the old religion, since it implied but the literal application of all the teachings of Christ." Filtering Tom Paine through Jonathan Edwards, Sinclair preaches about the redemption of "a man who was the world's first revolutionist, the true founder of the Socialist movement. . . . Who denounced in unmeasured terms the exploiters of his own time. . . . This union carpenter! This agitator, lawbreaker, firebrand, anarchist!"

Answering the objection of those who do not believe in democratic socialism, Sinclair guaranteed the achievement of American equality through a rational distribution of wealth *without* totalitarian thought control:

There was only one earth, and the quantity of material things was limited. Of intellectual and moral things, on the other hand, there was no limit, and one could have more without another's having less; hence "Communism in material production, anarchism in intellectual," was the formula of modern proletarian thought.

Sinclair's answer to the immigrants' problem applies the old solution, democracy, to the new conditions, industrialization and the emergence of mass man. Instead of the pathetic marriage of old immigrant values and new economic frustrations, Sinclair's solution insures that the survival of the fittest will also mean the perpetuation of the best. For example, Jurgis gets his first job as a socialist because a socialist employer has fired a man for drinking too much. The implication is clear; while the capitalist system drives a man to drink, if one drinks under socialism one *earns* dismissal.

The American people could have had all this, in Sinclair's opinion, simply by voting for their own interests. And they settled for federal meat inspection. But if most Americans were unwilling to risk actualization of traditional ideas, Sinclair was more than willing to test his theories by putting his new financial resources to work in an experiment in cooperative living.

Whatever the ultimate shortcomings of *The Jungle*, it gave Sinclair $30,000 with which to finance Helicon Home Colony—an experiment in which Sinclair had a very personal interest. As he wrote later, "because Meta was almost out of her mind, and I did not know what to do with David, I started Helicon Hall."[14]

The property, which had previously been a boys' school, was described by the New York *Times* as palatial. It included a swimming pool, bowling alley, theater, and glass-protected tropical plants. Located on several acres of land in Englewood, New Jersey, the price was $36,000. Sinclair largely financed the effort, but other idealists were invited to contribute time, talent, and resources. Although plans called for hundreds of residents, twelve families spent the first winter in Helicon Hall, moving in on 1 November 1906. It was hoped that through experiment answers would evolve to some of the hotly debated questions of the day concerning child care, diet, and the right of women to participate in making decisions.[15]

In terms of public relations, Sinclair tried to emphasize the fact that this was only an effort at cooperative living, not a socialist colony. Anybody who believed, for example, that the usual methods of raising children, cooking food, and washing clothing were inefficient was invited to join—although a screening committee was set up to eliminate any applicants "whose habits and ideas would render them uncongenial." And with an eye toward compatibility, Sinclair's democratic ideals were compromised in the establishment of a rigid color line, "accepting the formula that the colony should be open to any white person of good moral character who is free from communicable disease."[16]

Possibly the public reference to communicable disease stimulated speculation about the sexual habits of the residents. More likely, the national reputation of socialists as virile experimenters made inevitable the rumors that Sinclair was running a "free love" nest. The man who blushed at the contemplation of Renaissance art was, of course, righteously indignant when he responded to these allegations in his *Autobiography*: "I do not know of any assemblage of forty adult persons where a higher standard of sexual morals prevailed than at Helicon Hall."

Sinclair Lewis came to tend the furnace. William James and John Dewey visited, exchanging theories with the colonists about psychic phenomena and education. In addition to participation in discussions about liberalism versus anarchism, Sinclair wrote *The Industrial Republic*, a book of prophecy that anticipated a social revolution "in America within one year after the Presidential election of 1912." The period spent in Helicon Hall was, in short, an optimistic time during which, Sinclair tells us in his *Autobiography*, "the young dreamer of Utopia lived according to his dreams." Then on 7 March 1907, Sinclair awakened to find Helicon Home Colony on fire. He escaped, to stand outside in the snow, watching the "beautiful utopia flame and roar, until it crashed in and died away to a dull glow."

After the rubble and the debts were cleared away, Sinclair returned to the familiar but unhappy state of affairs that had preceded publication of *The Jungle*. Stomach trouble and headaches returned with destitution. Meta almost died of appendicitis and was sent to a sanitarium in Battle Creek, Michigan, for recovery.

Upton joined her there later, and as a result of the argumentation of Dr. W. K. Kellogg—not as a result of his work on *The Jungle*—he became a vegetarian.

Very much interested in the health of his family, Sinclair decided to move to Bermuda for the winter of 1907–08. A publisher's advance for *The Metropolis* financed the trip, but poor sales meant Sinclair had to borrow money to return to the United States. *The Millenium*, a drama written in Bermuda, and *The Moneychangers* (a novel written as a sequel to *The Metropolis*) produced no significant interest and hardly enough income to cover Sinclair's minimal expenses. So when he received invitations to come to California from Gaylord Wilshire (the socialist gold miner) and poet George Sterling, Sinclair "set out over the pathway of the argonauts in a Pullman car."

Sinclair stopped at Chicago for a socialist rally, then moved on to the University of Kansas, where he wanted to meet a young writer with whom he had been corresponding. Sinclair was quite convinced that Harry Kemp would become the next great American poet. In fact, Kemp was to become the man whose relationship with Meta would provide scandalous copy for American gossip columns. In 1911, when Sinclair announced that he was going to seek a divorce, he was to blame Kemp with "influencing" Meta in the wrong ways.[17]

Sinclair spent the winter of 1908–09 in California, writing plays and trying to keep Sterling from drinking. (Meta was in New York with David, who had tonsillitis.) But by the spring of 1909, he and Meta agreed to try living together again. They met in Florida, neutral territory, moved to Long Island for the summer, and then went back to Battle Creek for the discovery of health through fasting, as described in *The Fasting Cure* (1911). Harry Kemp arrived to visit Upton, and while Harry was becoming interested in Meta, Sinclair made the acquaintance of Mary Craig Kimbrough, a twenty-five-year-old Southern belle from Mississippi.

Still interested in utopian experiments, Sinclair then moved his family to a single-tax colony in Alabama.* Shortly thereafter, agreeing to a divorce, Meta moved back north, leaving David with his father. Sinclair was writing his troubles into *Love's Pilgrimage* (1911), a book described in his *Autobiography* as "a novel about modern marriage that would show the possibility of a couple's agreeing to part, and still remaining friends."

In the spring of 1910 Upton and David Sinclair moved to another single-tax colony in Delaware. Meta joined them there, occupying one of three tents "on a strictly literary basis," until she moved south to help Mary Craig Kimbrough write a novel about the daughter of Jefferson Davis. Then Harry Kemp and George Sterling went east to visit at the same time as Meta and Mary Craig went north to negotiate with publishers, and the stage was set for a public divorce scandal.

Sinclair, the notorious troublemaker, was subjected to vicious analyses of his own troubles. In *The Brass Check* he reports that the "generally accepted explanation was that I had married an innocent young girl and taught her 'free love' doctrines, and then, when she

---

* The single-tax method of solving all problems is usually associated with the nineteenth-century American political economist Henry George. In *Letters to Judd* (1926), Sinclair describes the effort to "take the burden of taxes off improvements, which are made by human labor, and put it on the land, which is the gift of Nature." But by 1926 Sinclair considered advocacy of a single tax to be a political blunder, since the poor saw it as a way for the rich to dodge taxes on bonds, jewelry, and other "improvements" on land.

practiced these doctrines, I kicked her out of my home."
Sinclair's own explanation, thinly fictionalized in *Love's Pilgrimage*, is less sensational but more perceptive. He has Thyrsis write a letter to Mr. Hardin, Corydon's new love:

I suppose there is no need for me to tell you that Corydon is not happy. She never has been happy as my wife, and I fear she never will be. She is by nature warm-hearted, craving affection and companionship. I, on the other hand, am by nature impersonal and self-absorbed—I am compelled by the exigencies of my work to be abstracted and indifferent to things about me. . . . If in the course of time it should become clear that Corydon would be happier as your wife than as mine, I should regard it as my duty to step aside.

But divorces were granted more easily by Thyrsis than by Catholic judges in New York at that time. So in 1912 Sinclair went to Amsterdam where "the husband was not required to prove that he had beaten or choked or poisoned his wife; he might receive a divorce on the basis of a signed statement by the wife, admitting infidelity."

Mary Craig followed Sinclair to the Netherlands, but their developing relationship was complicated by the awareness that Upton's friend, George Sterling, loved her too. Sterling wrote more than one hundred sonnets (which Sinclair later edited) to the woman whose "heart had been broken by an early love affair at home; she knew she would never love again." But she did, and then she persuaded her aristocratic father that she ought to marry a divorced man.

So the daughter of a Mississippi banker married the socialist muckraker on 21 April 1913. Until her death in 1961, Mary Craig was Sinclair's constant companion, providing consistent ideological support for an author whose personal life was always a large part of his writing.

This new marital situation provided the stability necessary for the continuing stream of liberal argument Sinclair was now prepared to address to an American public
—a reading audience that had misunderstood his first
significant novel but that would be given many more
chances to see how apparently dying American values
could be revitalized.

4

The Perpetual
Progressive

Feb. 22, 1930

Dear Sinclair:

I find your note on my return from Europe. As always, you are right—save in matters of politics, sociology, religion, finance, economics, literature, and the exact sciences.

—H. L. Mencken, in *My Lifetime in Letters.*

Once Sinclair had discovered, in his own mind, the relationship between American values and American capitalism, the crusader, as Walter Rideout concluded, made his life into "one long saga of St. George and the Dragon."[1] After spending the winter in Bermuda, Upton and Craig Sinclair returned to New York City in the spring of 1914, settling into a ten-dollar-a-week apartment on Morningside Heights. But nothing was settled in what Sinclair saw as the larger class struggle. Labor conditions in the coal mining areas of the Rocky Mountains provided the stimulus for Sinclair's next significant attack on the dragon of production for profit.

Major strikes had been going on during 1913 and 1914, but an event that came to be known as the Ludlow Massacre provoked Sinclair into action, both as an outraged citizen and as a novelist. Striking union members had set up tent colonies since they were not permitted to remain in the mining camps. Thugs, hired by the Colorado Fuel and Iron Company, doused the tents with kerosene, set them afire, and murdered three women and eleven children.

Sinclair believed that this event deserved more attention than the inch-long coverage given it by New York City papers, especially since the Colorado Fuel and Iron Company was controlled by a local citizen. So, with the support of four women, he conducted a silent protest "parade" outside the office of John D. Rockefeller, Jr. Arrested for "disorderly conduct," Sinclair's behavior proved more newsworthy than the original massacre. When he refused to pay the three dollar fine he was sentenced to three days in the Tombs, New York's less than modern prison. He discovered that if he served the entire sentence he would be unable to appeal the conviction, so he spent two days in fasting, paid one dollar, and continued the campaign after his release.

The demonstrations moved to Rockefeller's estate in Pocantico Hills. Then the conflict escalated. A bomb, apparently intended for Rockefeller, exploded prematurely in a tenement housing some members of the Industrial Workers of the World.* In an editorial praising the conviction of Sinclair, the New York *Times* contended that the "murderous plot and dynamite explosion" was a "direct consequence" of Sinclair's picket line.[2]

From his point of view, without endorsing violence, Sinclair argued in his *Autobiography* that the direct consequence of this series of events was a changed attitude in the Rockefeller family—beginning with the recognition of union demands by John D. Rockefeller, Jr. and continuing through the relatively liberal administration of Nelson Rockefeller as Governor of New York.

In any case, Sinclair visited Colorado four times to gather data about the working conditions of miners. Supported by sworn testimony taken under government supervision, Congressional Committee Reports, and a decision by the Colorado Supreme Court regarding fraudulent Colorado elections, Sinclair's novel, *King Coal* (1917), illustrated his belief that just as Rockefeller was to be held accountable for the Ludlow Massacre, the entire system of capitalism was to blame,

* This labor union, whose members were usually called Wobblies, was formed in 1905 as a radical alternative to the American Federation of Labor. The IWW hoped eventually to engage all the workers of the world in one big strike. Led by William D. Haywood and Elizabeth Gurley Flynn, the IWW had about 100,000 members at the peak of its strength. In 1917 the Justice Department made a concerted attack on the union, outlawing it and arresting over two hundred of its leaders. By the end of World War I, little was left of the movement. For Sinclair's sympathetic analysis of the Wobblies, see the fourteenth chapter of *Jimmie Higgins*.

ultimately, for conditions leading to the extended coal strikes.

Violence, in Sinclair's view, becomes inevitable when democratic avenues for change are closed as a matter of official policy. Class conflict will become combat when unions are not allowed to organize, when rights to public assembly are denied, when public elections are turned over to private corporations so that the ballots of illiterate voters can be marked for them by company officials.

The hero of *King Coal*, Hal Warner, is a college student born into the upper class. After countless dormitory arguments with less idealistic peers, Hal decides to investigate the living conditions of the sort of people who work for his sort of people. So he arrives, incognito, at a mining camp owned by the father of his colleague, Percy Harrigan. Since Hal is too clean and well-mannered to be a real miner, the camp marshall suspects he is a union organizer; his application is turned down. When Hal sneaks into camp anyway, he is beaten, robbed, and warned not to return.

Looking a bit more like a regular miner as a result of his reception, Hal learns from hoboes that in order to get a job at a mine one needs connections. He agrees to give a saloonkeeper a dollar a month for an introduction to a friend inside the camp who will get him hired (for an additional monthly half dollar). Going by the name of Joe Smith, Hal is hired to take care of the underground mule stables, a demeaning job that, after "deductions" plus "board" and "room," leaves him with fourteen dollars per month.

But Hal is enterprising and shortly learns that he can receive a better job by paying a foreman fifteen of the twenty-five dollars to be earned via the promotion.

The miserable conditions of mining work, the effective slave system of the company store, and the debilitating anesthetic of alcohol, are all portrayed for the reader as Hal learns what it means to be a miner.

It becomes increasingly clear to Hal that the only solution is to form a union. For individual initiative means paying off a foreman to assign one to a rich vein in a system that pays men by the amount of coal dug rather than by the hour. Far from becoming a revolutionist, Hal concludes that actual enforcement of *current* laws regarding working hours, safety conditions, and union organization would be satisfactory. But the enforcers of law are on the company payrolls too. An explosion, necessary to attract public attention, is inevitable—on the literal level because the company refuses to spend the money to equip the mines with a sprinkling system, on the larger level because of contradictions built into capitalist greed.

In *King Coal*, Sinclair charges that when a mine catches fire the mine is sealed—suffocating the fire (and the men trapped below) before it can burn much of the resource material. More than one hundred men are caught in the incident Sinclair narrates, and Hal rushes to town to get the newspapers to publish accounts of the disaster before it is too late. But the powerful papers are not eager to malign the most powerful employer in the area.

Fortunately, a special train carrying young Percy Harrigan is passing through town. Hal, closely pursued by the camp marshal, bursts into the car and convinces Percy to unseal his father's mine.

This, of course, solves only the immediate problem. But at the end of the book the union that Hal has helped to organize agrees to remain secret until the

United Mine Workers have organized all the surrounding camps. Then, and only then, will the anticipated strike be effective.

While researching and writing *King Coal*, Sinclair was also busy compiling *The Cry For Justice*, an anthology of protest literature. It was published in 1915, the same year in which the Sinclairs established themselves permanently in California. In addition, throughout these years Sinclair was gathering data for a series of books that attempted to expose the corruptness of basic American institutions—the church (*The Profits of Religion*), the press (*The Brass Check*), and the schools (*The Goose-step, The Goslings*).

But before he could continue his attack on the system, Sinclair had to confront a basic issue. What does a social reformer do when the society to be reformed is threatened with collapse? More precisely, what does an American socialist do when confronted by an international situation steadily degenerating into World War I? Sinclair joined his Dutch friend, Fredrick van Eeden, in the formation of the International League—a coalition of intellectuals attempting to "stave off" the war.[3] But as this sort of effort failed, as it became clear that America would enter the European conflict, Sinclair felt increasingly alienated from a Socialist Party that continued to argue that American workers had no reason to help British capitalists fight German capitalists.

In July of 1917 major newspapers printed Sinclair's letter of resignation from the Socialist Party, a letter which contended that "the ability to think consists in the discovery of differences in things which appear alike. . . . It is fatally easy to say that all capitalist governments are alike, and that all must be opposed in the same way."[4]

As would be expected, Sinclair's personal concerns

show up in his publications. He depicts the dilemma faced by American socialists quite effectively in *Jimmie Higgins* (1919)—a novel offered for the contemplation of those who consider Sinclair completely simple-minded. For in this book no obvious solutions are proposed. The direction Jimmie eventually moves in turns out to be ideologically and personally disastrous. And no alternatives emerge to indicate that Jimmie could have done something better.

Jimmie Higgins, who at age nineteen (with ten years of hobo life behind him) marries a good-hearted prostitute, is shown at the beginning of the novel as the indispensable, but not too bright, stalwart who does the menial work at the local level of socialist politics. At the high point of his career he accidently meets The Candidate (obviously Eugene V. Debs), who draws strength and inspiration from Jimmie's dedication to the cause.

Jimmie could agree completely with The Candidate's contention that the world was entering its "blackest of calamities" because capitalism always needs to expand, needs new markets for its surplus products, and needs war industry to keep its wage slaves employed. But what, on a personal level, does all this mean for Jimmie? Through vivid descriptions of debates carried on in the weekly meetings of the socialist local, Sinclair outlines the alternatives open to Jimmie.

To support Germany's hope for American neutrality would be to damage the imperialistic countries of France and England—but also to support the imperialistic Kaiser. Still, some German socialists were arguing that only after Germany controlled and organized the chaos of Europe could a socialist reorganization take place. And the Bolshevik leaders of the Russian Revolution seemed willing to combat Germany with propaganda rather than arms. So Jimmie tended to remain neutral, with his inclinations toward German victory supported by the many Germans in his local.

But neutrality becomes increasingly difficult to maintain. No matter where Jimmie worked, he contributed to a capitalist economy that was beginning to engage in war production. To complicate the issue, America was becoming intolerant of the neutrality advocated by socialists. Speakers were jailed, newspapers were barred from the mails, and Jimmy was led to wonder about the validity of "fighting for Democracy abroad, if you had to sacrifice every particle of Democracy at home in order to win the fight."

Then the German armies attacked Russia, and to Jimmie's disbelief German socialists obeyed their Prussian officers when ordered to fire on the red flag. Frustrated and angry, Jimmie enlists—perfectly aware that in fighting the Germans who were fighting the Bolsheviks, he would be helping the French bankers who had loaned four billion dollars to the Czar. But President Wilson was promising the world that this would be the last necessary battle for democracy. And Jimmie anticipated a return to normal socialist agitation as soon as America brought this international idiocy to a mandatory end.

As a motorcycle repairman, Jimmie is sent to deliver a message to a French battery on the front lines. He is sucked into the combat, shooting a gun for the first time in his life, and receiving a serious arm wound in his determined effort to guarantee democracy by "licking 'em Heinies."

Sinclair, as the author of this sort of propaganda, found that socialist publications were unwilling to publish his defense of American policy. So in 1918 he began his own magazine, *Upton Sinclair's: For a Clean Peace and the Internation*. While publishing *Jimmie Higgins*

in serial form in this magazine, Sinclair's enthusiasm
began to sour, and he turned the end of his novel into
another direction.

A recovered hero emerges from the hospital as Ser-
geant Jimmie Higgins, convinced that his earlier pacifism
was entirely impractical, and thrilled to learn that he is
being sent to a port in northern Russia. Then he discovers that his expedition is to fight the Bolsheviks rather
than the Germans. "And Jimmie Higgins, under martial
law, must obey and hold his tongue."

This he cannot do for long. Arrested for distributing
among Americans the same tracts that the Bolsheviks
had used to discourage Germans from attacking them,
Jimmie is tortured by American military police when he
refuses to name the Russian source of the propaganda.
Hung by his thumbs and given the "water-cure," Jimmie's loyalty to socialism does not crack, but his mind
does. The reader's last view of Jimmie reveals a barking,
growling creature who gnaws off the ends of his fingers
just as wild animals chew off their own limbs to escape
from a trap.

Sinclair too was trapped by the position he had felt
forced to take during the war. Ten years after his resignation from the Socialist Party, embittered at the agreement Wilson signed in Paris, Sinclair admitted his error:

. . . if at the beginning of 1917 I had known what I know
today, I would have opposed the war and gone to jail with
the pacifist radicals. . . . I cannot forgive him [Wilson]; it
is not merely that he made a fool of himself, but he made a
fool of me![5]

So in 1920 he wrote *100%, The Story of a Patriot*,
a caustic satire about a labor-union spy. Although not a
significant novel, *100%* shows Sinclair dropping his
defense of the American government and returning to

his more familiar role of critic. But Sinclair's primary
attack during these years was to be made outside the
realm of fiction. While changing his mind about Jimmie
Higgins, he was solidifying long-held opinions about the
American church. In 1918 he presented *The Profits of
Religion*, a "Study of Supernaturalism . . . as a Source of
Income & a Shield to Privilege."

Drawing his examples from the Old Testament, the
Inquisition, and his own observations, Sinclair concluded
that institutionalized religion, based on the exploitation
of human fears, could be counted upon to oppose all
progressive changes—whatever, whenever, wherever.
After tracing the history of the Anglican church in this
respect, he pays special attention to Roman Catholicism
—a religion with a basic tenet of "obey and keep silence," a religion with an educational system constructed
to prevent education. Sinclair quotes Pius IX to the
effect that "liberty of conscience is a most pestiferous
error, from which arises revolution, corruption, contempt
of sacred things, holy institutions, and laws." Luther
may have reformed religion, but so far as Sinclair could
see, Luther's attitude toward German peasant revolts
retold the same old story. And it established the tone
for a religion admirably suited to become the state
church of Prussia.

After pressing his attack on all the established
churches, Sinclair switches to the more humorous but
equally reactionary "quacks." Seventh-day Adventists,
Mormons, Holy Rollers, and Christian Scientists, all
practice the "Graft of Grace," which turns poor prophets
into wealthy charlatans.

Sinclair concludes his long sermon with his own
altar call. To join "the Church of the Social Revolution"
is to follow the attack of Jesus Christ on the defenders
of privilege.

Two years later, in 1920, Sinclair extended his systems analysis to the fourth estate. While the American Revolution may have insured political freedom of the press, to function within capitalism means to exchange that ideal freedom for the right to advertise. Taking his title, *The Brass Check*, from the metal token paid to cheap whores after services rendered, the book outlines Sinclair's experiences with American journalism.

Sinclair uses *Everybody's* as an example of a magazine that used muckraking articles to attract a large audience, then moved to steadily more conservative positions in order to retain advertisers. Similarly influenced, newspapers always had plenty of space to relate gossip about Sinclair's "love nests" and "divorce scandals," but a censorship of silence was applied to really newsworthy events such as the Ludlow Massacre. Since our newspapers are owned by private interests, argued Sinclair, one cannot even hope that they will work for the public good. Journalism has become

one of the devices whereby industrial autocracy keeps its control over political democracy; it is the day-by-day, between-elections propaganda, whereby the minds of the people are kept in a state of acquiescence, so that when the crisis of an election comes, they go to the polls and cast their ballots for either one of the two candidates of their exploiters. Not hyperbolically and contemptuously, but literally and with scientific precision, we define Journalism in America as the business and practice of presenting the news of the day in the interest of economic privilege.

Sinclair did not believe that America's power elite was entirely monolithic. Some honest reporting occurs, from time to time, when contending parties make war on each other. But this, though refreshing, only indicates business interests opposing other business interests. Basing his case on hundreds of illustrations, Sinclair

concluded that under current conditions no periodical
or newspaper would be allowed to argue effectively and
consistently against the very business of business.

Once again, Sinclair's solutions follow from his outline of the problem. Laws should be passed requiring
papers to correct statements, when proved false, with the
same prominence given the original charge. Cities, rather
than individuals, should own newspapers. Journalists
should form a national union. And a national weekly,
financed through subscription, should become a chronicle of events, with no editorials or advertisements.

The New York *Times*, not surprisingly, printed an
attack on *The Brass Check*, launched by Dr. James
Melvin Lee, Director of the Department of Journalism
of New York University. Lee pointed out that Sinclair
had lied to the public before, signing the name of
Arthur Stirling to a book he had written himself. *The
Brass Check*, he argued, was a hoax of similar quality.
But in an editorial of 29 March 1921, the *Times* refused
to grant Sinclair space to answer Lee, for the editors
agreed with Lee that Sinclair was dishonest. In the official view, then, it "may be mildly interesting to watch
Mr. Lee swatting a fly, but there is no reason why any
of the spectators should open his house as a refuge for
the pestiferous and defiling insect."

But within two years the pest returned, armed with
a massive indictment charging the defilement of another
American institution supposedly dedicated to free expression—higher education. Beginning once again with personal experience, in *The Goose-Step* (1923) Sinclair
describes his uneducational experience at The House of
Morgan (Columbia University).

He then sets the pattern for the book by describing
the interlocking directorship of a university administered

by the same men who run major business and for the same reasons. After identifying the trustees by name and corporation, Sinclair devotes special attention to Columbia's President, Nicholas Murray Butler. From Butler's goose-stepping support of the Kaiser in 1907, quoted by Sinclair, emerges the title of the book. American education, far from free inquiry, constitutes the systematic indoctrination of our youth, "not to further the welfare of mankind, but merely to keep America capitalist."

Sinclair sent out a mail survey to more than one hundred American professors, but they were marching in goosestep, too worried about their own jobs to help a muckraker with his. So Sinclair did his own research, visiting about thirty schools across the country, traveling more than seven thousand miles to hold confidential interviews with professors. Neither geographical setting nor the level of academic prestige seemed to affect the power structures of our colleges and universities. Neither church affiliation nor support from state taxes seemed to guarantee academic freedom. Since the main weakness of Sinclair's book is his repetition of the same case too many dozen times, one example will suffice to show what Sinclair discovered. At Northwestern University, the

first vice-president of the university is the general counsel of the Illinois Steel Company; the third vice-president is vice-president of the Illinois Steel Company; while the grand duke is the very grandest of all grand dukes in the United States—that prince of open shoppers and potentate of reaction, Judge Gary, chairman of the United States Steel Corporation!

Sinclair had a fine time on his tour. University officials often provided an illustration of his thesis by refusing to let him speak on campus, thus engendering

public interest and free advertisement. To keep himself
physically fit, he played tennis. He was delighted to
report that at the University of Wisconsin he "met the
champion tennis team . . . and played each of its members in turn, and beat them in straight sets." He was
told "that the student body regarded this as a far more
sensational incident than my Socialist speech." He lost
to the team captain at the University of Chicago (The
University of Standard Oil), but according to the student newspaper quoted by Sinclair, "he did it with a
grace that does not characterize his books and speeches."

Sinclair's concept of free academic institutions had
no room for the widespread discrimination practiced
against Jews, the new importance of athletics, or the
growth of departments that taught trades (business, journalism, education) instead of liberal arts.

His solutions, hopefully obvious to veteran readers
and professors, included a labor union for teachers, university constitutions to provide government by faculty,
alumni, and students, and "workers colleges" (very
similar to what are now called "free universities").

Few were surprised when Sinclair returned the following year with *The Goslings*, a volume illustrating his
contention that big business also oils the educational
machine at lower production levels. Again, although Sinclair emphasizes Los Angeles, New York, and Chicago,
it makes little difference whether he is discussing the
situation in Boston, Massachusetts, or Big Timber,
Montana. The same realtors, manufacturers, physicians,
lawyers, and wives of the rich sit on school boards that
produce similar rulings on the rights of students to hear
certain sorts of speakers and the rights of married women
to be teachers. Throughout the country, Sinclair found,
women did the work for which male administrators were
paid. Librarians had been fired with a leer for refusing to

buy Liberty bonds. ("Would you want a German to ravish you?")

In Philadelphia 74% of the school buildings were not fireproof, toilet facilities were unsanitary, and the schools were so crowded that 40,000 students were forced onto part-time schedules. In St. Louis things were even worse because Catholics ran the school system.

Sinclair's solution, like the problem, was repetitious. A teachers' union was mandatory. It would be futile, he felt, to try to work through the National Education Association, since that organization was controlled by supervisors.

From 1918 to 1924, then, Sinclair wrote four books that attempted to provide enormous documentation of the basic message he had been delivering in his fiction. American society was being mismanaged from above; without revolutionary violence, the people could correct that situation with votes from below. And Sinclair was determined to practice what he had been preaching.

Warming up for his later and more serious attempts to gain political office, Sinclair rejoined the Socialist Party and took the time and energy to run as its candidate—for Congress in 1920, for the U. S. Senate in 1922, and for Governor of California in 1926 and 1930. His success was slight. In the 1922 Senate race, for example, he received 37,476 votes. This gave him fourth place, far behind the Republican winner and Democratic and Prohibition also-rans.[6]

Not all of Sinclair's causes were doomed to failure. In 1923 he won a libel suit against the former Premier of Austria. For calling him "a knave" in a book review, Dr. Max Hussarck was required by a Viennese jury to pay Sinclair 500,000 crowns, about $100,000.[7]

That same year a more important success, the founding of the American Civil Liberties Union in

southern California, resulted from another Sinclair
arrest. Civil libertarians such as Sinclair were outraged
at the plans of city officials in Los Angeles to respond
to a waterfront strike by "housing" I.W.W. members in
a stockade. In his desire for open-air meetings to discuss
the issue, Sinclair was arrested for "conspiracy to commit
a breach of the peace and obstruct traffic."[8] In fact, as
Sinclair claims in his *Autobiography*, he was guilty of
trying "to read the Constitution of the United States at
a meeting on private property." The *Nation* gave the
incident wide publicity; Police Chief Louis Oaks was
fired; and the A.C.L.U., in Sinclair's judgment, "put an
end to the oppression of labor in California. . . ."

By preaching and attempting to practice his liberalism in such a consistent way, Sinclair earned Frederick
Hoffman's amazing tribute: "Upton Sinclair proved to
be the sole active survivor of progressive liberalism in
the twenties. . . ."[9] By enjoying his life as perpetual
progressive so much, Sinclair the Crusader also earned
an equally amazing tribute from a social critic who
rarely bought what Sinclair was selling. In a letter to
Sinclair (28 January 1920), H. L. Mencken commented:
"To hell with Socialism! The longer I live the more I
am convinced that the common people are doomed to
be diddled forever. You are fighting a vain fight. But you
must be having a lot of fun."

Sinclair had so much fun with his next significant
novel, *Oil!*, that the book was banned in Boston upon
publication in 1927. This was an honor that the writer,
who called himself the "prize prude of the radical movement,"[10] had never anticipated. But Sinclair did not
neglect a perfect publicity gimmick. As his introduction
to the book advertises, "I had a printer black out the
offending passages [dealing with birth control] with fig
leaves and then I sold the books on Boston Common,

and everybody had a good laugh at the police who
arrested me."

The novel opens with a long description of J. Arnold
Ross and his young son, Bunny, driving through the
Guadalupe Pass toward Beach City, California, the site
of a recent discovery of oil. Dad Ross, an independent
oil operator, represents the best of the self-made men in
1912; Bunny is a sensitive boy, trying to make sense of
the world he will later inherit. Bunny will mature in the
course of the book, which means he will come to Sinclair's conclusions about sex, the movies, college, and
capitalism.

Bunny views the same American Dream from a
vantage point opposite to that of Jurgis Rudkus. As
a son of success, he knows that he will never have to
struggle to survive economically. The American economic system, which defeats an angry Jurgis, makes
Bunny feel guilty. Carefully setting up his character
types, Sinclair turns Bunny into a sketch of the American liberal caught in the dilemma of an idealist who
sees many of his social values as conflicting with the
ultimate value—pragmatism. The American liberal's
quandary becomes a dominant theme from this point on
in Sinclair's fiction, a chronicle of frustration examined
with great care, from the inside.

Consider J. Arnold Ross, the positive result of the
American experiment. A financial success, his concept of
"a world you had to help yourself in" has little room for
boyish interest in existential mysteries. Bunny imagines
that the experience of being pulled over a "magic ribbon
of concrete" by "the power of ninety horses" is rather
glorious. "What magic had done this?" he asks, child-
ishly. And Sinclair, through Dad, gives capitalism's satisfied response: "money had done it." As usual, Sinclair
makes sure that his point is not missed:

Out of the clouds overhead a great bird came sailing; his wings collapsed as if he had been shot, and he dived into the abyss. "Was that an eagle?" asked the boy. "Buzzard," answered Dad, who had no romance in him.

Always associated with the automobile, Dad's mechanistic concept of success is personified by the sound of his horn, which was "sharp and military; there was in it no undertone of human kindness." A hard, but respectful, user of machinery, Dad drives sixty miles per hour, even when he has chains on, but he stops regularly to grease the automobile out of allegiance to "the general principle of doing things right, of paying respect to a beautiful piece of machinery." But that respect is also based on economic values: " 'Grease is cheaper than steel,' Dad would say."

Not a simple villain, Dad represents the best that a capitalist ethic has to offer. Influenced increasingly by Bunny, his attitude toward his employees is generally benevolent, but his concept of reality differs from that of his son. When workers stay out on strike too long, Dad will yield to pressures from other oil men to hire scab labor; business is business. Bunny's mind, on the other hand, "was all one compartment; things ought to be right, and if they were not right, you ought to *make* them right, or else what was the use of having any right —you were only fooling yourself about it."

This continual conflict between father and son is balanced in the novel by a parallel disagreement between Bunny and Paul, the young man Bunny admires most. Representing the other side of the capital versus labor dialectic, Paul is very much like Dad. As a professional labor organizer, he too is rather coldly analytical. Paul and Dad respect each other and share a mutual definition of self-interest. They discuss real subjects, such as scientific knowledge. Their common concept of pragmatism wonders:

why didn't Bunny study biology and physics, instead of letting them fill his head up with Latin and poetry, and history business about old kings and their wars and their mistresses, that wasn't a bit of use to nobody?

Bunny loves them both, even as they gradually accept the need to fight each other to the death.

Bunny's liberal dilemma is based on his perplexing ability to see both sides of all issues. When Dad and Vernon Roscoe—the capitalist who takes Dad's ethics to their logical conclusion—decide to purchase Senator Warren G. Harding as the Republican candidate for President, Bunny understands that they are merely practicing free enterprise. "And then, a few hours later, he would . . . sit down with Paul . . . and the rest of the 'Bolshevik bunch,' and see too clearly why they wanted the oil workers to organize and educate themselves, and take over the oil wells from Dad and Mr. Roscoe!" Essentially, the plot development of the novel shows Bunny "making such earnest and devoted efforts to ride on two horses at once! And the horses kept getting farther and farther apart, until he was all but split in the middle."

Although Sinclair's sympathies are obviously with Bunny, he points candidly to the weaknesses of the liberal stance. Bunny, the social reformer like Sinclair, induces his father to provide green plants in reading rooms established for the edification of the workers. Then Bunny, the liberal, evaluates his own behavior as "growing roses on the barbed wire fence which separated capital from labor."

Vernon Roscoe's opinion comes from the other

direction, but it amounts to the same advice that Bunny receives regularly from Paul: "What I tell you is, you better get on your own side of the fence before the shooting begins." These views, which endorse looking out for one's self-interest, fail to see the complications of the liberal perspective. For the self-interest of the liberal amounts to nothing less than the establishment of a world of well-meaning and effective people living within a democratic society where all differences are resolved within dialogue.

Bunny, who advocates achieving this goal in a peaceable manner, tends to accept the analysis from the left that claims that conservative forces are primarily to blame for inhibiting that step-by-step approach to a sane society. But the left is not faultless. In some of the most effective passages in *Oil!* Bunny also sees the socialist movement split into factions that attack each other with the same passion they direct toward their supposedly common enemy. All of this confusion he tries to fit into his liberal faith in the ability of the human race to progress.

To complicate the issue still more, Bunny is aware of the pernicious effect of personal interest upon his analysis. Achieving the desired social order is to his self-interest in the long run, because he would no longer have to carry the burden of guilt felt by every liberal American who knows that his relative affluence is based on the misery of others. Since Bunny believes that "the whole world was one elaborate system, opposed to justice and kindness, and set to making cruelty and pain," his private successes on the gridirons of college and bed only make him feel more guilty:

Yes, even when Bunny was up in the snow-white room with the ivy vines wreathing the window, even while he held in his arms the eager body of his beloved—even then the prison door would clang, and he would be in a tank of the county jail with the "class-war prisoners!"

Liberal shame increases because the prisons are only mental. In a land where self-reliance is deified, Bunny inherits the social position that keeps him out of jail and, when accompanied by good looks, stimulates enterprising women to leap into his arms. He has everything, has earned nothing, and understands all sides of all issues.

Thus, while it is to his long-range interest to ease guilt feelings by achieving economic equality, his immediate desires always pressure Bunny to keep things exactly as they are. Coeducational acrobatics with Hollywood starlets between satin sheets are conducive to a good night's sleep. An equally important love for his father leads to resentment of strikes that give owners ulcers.

Much of the energy of the novel, consequently, is expended in running away from long-range liberal self-interest at the behest of short-range concerns. And the flight is never successful. Bunny's grand tour of Europe includes breakfasts in beds shared with a film starlet. Together they read accounts of movie premieres, reminding themselves of "who had attended and what they had worn. And then, turning over the paper, Bunny read a dispatch from Angel City—ten thousand oil workers had walked out on strike. . . ."

Psychologically, the alternative escapes for the liberal mentality seem to be sentimental nostalgia for the good old days or cynical acceptance of the present. Implicit in the conclusion that "the land of the pilgrim's pride no longer existed" is the belief that things were different once. Even Dad feels a need for a periodic escape from industrialized success. So father and son attempt to return to nature on hunting trips that are geared toward relieving the anxieties of the machine age.

The millionaire hunter who is a poor shot will not be rewarded in the primitive world where competition is pure, without complications.

But this is twentieth-century America, the land of opportunity for any endeavor except a return to the past. When Dad and Bunny go hunting, Bunny discovers oil oozing out of the ground, and the whole area is eventually turned into the money-making success story from which they are hunting relief.

The other option, cynicism, was one widely adopted by Sinclair's liberal peers in the 1920s. Woodrow Wilson, who had made a fool of Sinclair with respect to World War I, emerges in *Oil!* as a character who gives parts of Germany to France and Italy, parts of Africa to England, and parts of China to Japan—all in the name of self-determination. Sinclair blames Wilson for "a tone of hilarious cynicism [which] became the correct thing among the young intellectuals of America." Shown to be as disastrous as the attempt to return to earlier ages through hunting, the cynical response to modern dilemmas leads logically to the buying and selling of the American presidency, making an expensive joke of the process that that office represents.

Taking the only other apparent alternative, Bunny continues to muddle along, aware of the contradictions in his own behavior, hoping Americans will finally learn that to accept capitalism means to reject the other values basic to the American experiment.

Dominant American culture, because of capitalism, is trash. The entertainment industry, symbolized by Hollywood in this novel, is based on the casting couch, where women become whores in a way explicitly connected by Sinclair to the larger capitalist conspiracy that forces workers to sell themselves too cheaply. Vee Tracy (Bunny's Hollywood flame), in the opinion of Rachel

Menzies (Bunny's socialist comrade and eventual wife), is "nothing but a prostitute." Having sold her body to achieve stardom, Vee disgraces her sex by performing in a movie that is tantamount to propaganda for a war with Russia, a prospect Sinclair felt should be abhorrent to any normal American mother of normal American boys.

The effect of capitalism on education is similarly cheapening. College classes become exercises in trivia for Bunny, taught by professors who use their "spare time quite contentedly, counting the feminine endings [in the verses] in certain of the pre-Elizabethan dramatists." The scientists sell themselves too. Dad chuckles while remembering his hiring of "a chemical wizard, paying him six thousand a year, and making millions out of him!" Controlling the masses as effectively as the elites, education serves capitalism by staging weekly combats between hired gladiators—athletes disguised as students—in order to distract the attention of the workers away from their own class conflicts.

Although learning little about socialism in college classes, Bunny's [Sinclair's] study of the liberal role in world affairs helps him learn from the radical left that there is a solution:

Bunny, confronting the modern industrial world with its manifold injustices, had been like a man lost in a tangled forest. But here he had been taken up in a balloon, and shown the way out of the tangle. Everything was now simple, plain as a map. The workers were to take over the industries, and run them for themselves, instead of for masters. Thus, with one stroke, the knot of social injustice would be cut!

If this sounds very much like the experience of Jurgis, it should be remembered that the author of *Oil*!

still considered America a "fairyland turned into a
slaughterhouse, where the many were ground up into
sausages for the breakfast of the few." And again Sinclair rejects the analysis of the radical left when he has
Bunny reject (with hesitation and sympathy) Paul's conclusion that successful revolution necessarily involves violence.

And Bunny survives, whereas Paul and Dad die of
their own chosen responses to the American illness.
While it might be more noble to die the martyr's death
of Paul, and while it might seem to be more comfortable
to be outwardly successful while rotting away from the
inside like Dad, really heroic confrontation of modern
society, in Sinclair's view, is the approach chosen by the
American liberal. All evidence to the contrary, Bunny is
still a believer in the possibility of turning the American
dream into a reality—despite awareness of personal weaknesses, despite ideological contradictions, and despite all
the persuasive data gathered by those on both sides of
the barbed-wire fence on which the liberal uncomforta-
bly sits out the struggle.

Bunny and Rachel form a labor college;[11] contemporary education and the current propaganda of the
movie industry have led Bunny into trouble, but that
does not mean that the ideals of education and propaganda should be dropped. They remain tools, to be used
by Sinclair in the fight against the "evil Power which
roams the earth, crippling the bodies of men and women,
and luring the nations to destruction by visions of
unearned wealth and the opportunity to enslave and
exploit labor."

Having ended *Oil!* with a statement of faith
addressed to a disillusioned generation, Sinclair returned
to his analysis of the liberal dilemma the next year. In
Boston (1928), Sinclair runs his liberal protagonist

through another confrontation between radical critics and the conservative supporters of the established order.

The arrest of two Italians, Nicola Sacco and Bartolomeo Vanzetti, in May of 1920, triggered a series of events that caused American liberals to question the viability of their own point of view. Charged with robbery and murder, it became obvious to many that the men were really to be tried and eventually executed for their political ideas, a shocking prospect in the land of free expression. "Like lightning," writes literary critic Sherman Paul, "the case of the Italian anarchists had cracked throughout the decade."[12] Walter Rideout agrees about the impact of the case: "Writers, the seismographs of social shock, recorded—and still record—the profound disturbance. . . . But the important point is that the whole intellectual community, of which writers are a part, was eventually dislocated by the shock. . . ."[13] Edmund Wilson, one of the leading writers within that community, describes the execution of 1927 as the event which "made liberals lose their bearings."[14]

Although Sinclair joined other writers—John Dos Passos, Mike Gold, Edna St. Vincent Millay, Katherine Anne Porter, Zona Gale, Carl Van Doren, Dorothy Parker, Ida M. Tarbell—in vigorous protest against what Edmund Wilson called a "judicial lynching," *Boston* reveals a writer whose examination of the Sacco-Vanzetti case reinforced rather than upset his liberal point of view. Through Cornelia Thornwell, Sinclair considers and then rejects the anarchist solution to the injustice of American capitalism.

Mixing history with imagination in what he called a "contemporary historical novel," in his preface Sinclair offered a simple formula to readers interested in separating fact from fiction: "The characters who are real persons bear real names, while those who bear ficti-

tious names are fictitious characters." With respect to
fact, Louis Joughin and Edmund M. Morgan, historians
of the Sacco-Vanzetti case, have praised *Boston* without
serious reservation:

It is accurate in detail to the degree that one would expect
of a scientific study, and it has qualities of proportion in its
judgments which indicate careful thinking. This combination of completeness, accuracy, and penetration places *Boston*
in the first rank of historical novels.[15]

Sinclair's technique is familiar. Again, making use
of all available information—including a 3,900-page trial
transcript—he invites the reader to conclude that his
political judgments are as demonstrable as the documented facts. And these judgments pertain to the person really on trial in *Boston*—the American liberal. Sacco
and Vanzetti, in Sinclair's presentation, are clearly innocent in that they have not been proved guilty of robbery
or murder. The real concern of the novel, then, is the
inability of American liberalism to deal with the sort of
stress symbolized by the Sacco-Vanzetti affair.

The burden of a liberal perspective is placed, in
this book, on the aging shoulders of Sinclair's heroine,
Cornelia Thornwell, whose domineering husband Josiah
—twice elected Governor of Massachusetts—starts the
plot moving with his own death. Cornelia, like Bunny,
could live happily ever after, with finances and good
name insured by the American system. But although
she is sixty, she decides that she still has time to live
her own life at last. So she leaves her daughters to squab-
ble over the relics of her husband and drops off Boston's
society pages into the next-door world of the immigrant
laborer.

Determined to see if she can survive on her own,
she gets a menial job at a factory in Plymouth, renting a

cheap room from an Italian family. The other lodger there is Vanzetti, an anarchist who hates all bosses (whether capitalist or labor union) but who, like Jurgis, had brought a dream with him to America: " 'Hear about Statue Liberty—beautifool, wonderfool—paradiso. Come Ellis Island, all sudden knock on head, like badda dream, inferno—brutale, treat people lika beast—little ones cry, hide in modder's dress.' " These are new insights for Cornelia, who becomes close friends with Vanzetti as the months, troubles, and strikes go by.

After one year, Cornelia accidently meets Betty, her favorite grandchild, on the street. The two agree to keep Cornelia's experiment secret, but Betty's parents discover letters, and they arrive to take Cornelia back to respectability. A long negotiating session leads to an agreement; Cornelia will quit her job, leaving Plymouth for a proper apartment in Boston, and Betty will live with her.

Sinclair uses the relationship between Betty and Cornelia to portray the closeness of liberal and leftist ideology. For having been introduced to socialist and anarchist thought by meeting Cornelia's working-class friends, Betty soon moves past Cornelia's position to that of revolutionary communism. Representing a pure but immature idealism, Betty is treated sympathetically by Sinclair; but his novel ultimately sides once again with the social democrat, Cornelia, who "did not want Betty to go with the fighting crowd."

Cornelia and Betty decide to visit the Soviet Union to check on the condition of women living under socialism. Cornelia returns to give lectures on the subject, and she becomes active in the movement to defend immigrants who were being deported by the hundreds because of leftist affiliations. The work is exhausting, so Cornelia decides to take a vacation, meeting Betty in Italy. While

there, they learn of the arrest of Vanzetti. So they
return to take up the task that occupies them throughout
the rest of this long novel, the attempt to hold the
American legal system to its promise of justice for all.

The Sacco-Vanzetti case, although interesting in its
own right, serves Sinclair as an occasion for his continuing interest in the American liberal's predicament. Sacco
barely enters the narrative. He is considered a "primitive
mind," and he might even be guilty of the crimes as
charged, though the case is not proved. Vanzetti develops
social theories that receive Sinclair's detailed attention.
But *Boston* remains Cornelia's story. An important sub-
plot, for example, exposes the pettiness, deceit, graft,
and thievery of respected members of her family—with
the treatment they receive in America's legal channels
contrasting sharply with that given the anarchists.

Cornelia, a leader in the committee set up to insure a
fair trial for men who do not believe in committees, is
shocked to learn that for $50,000 she can have the case
dropped. Although the task of raising such amounts
would be relatively easy in her circles, she refuses out of
principle and is supported by the equally pure Vanzetti.
Their lawyer agrees with their position, because he
believes he has an ideal case to test freedom of opinion
in America. But he later sees that he will lose the case,
and he then encourages Cornelia to lie for the cause by
swearing that she was with Vanzetti at the time of the
crime. Perjury from an aristocrat, he will argue, is more
convincing to a jury than the honest statements of many
Italians who bought eels from Vanzetti during that
crucial day.

Having learned much about the lower classes by
working with them, Cornelia now gains new insights into
the quality of the conservative circles she had lived
within for years. Harvard's President Lowell, in charge

of a citizens' committee reviewing the case, and Governor Fuller are both given opportunities to reverse or modify the findings of an obviously prejudiced trial judge. Sinclair's novel dramatizes the historical verdict of Joughin and Morgan: "The terrible truth of the Sacco-Vanzetti case is that the official representatives of New England culture sanctioned the sending of two men to their death in the face of reasonable doubt."[16]

The American liberal faces the classic moral dilemma concerning means and ends here. Cornelia becomes increasingly aware of the willingness of the state to intimidate witnesses, falsify records, and eliminate contradictory evidence. She has to decide whether or not to fight vicious and damaging lies with a benevolent lie of her own: "When Cornelia remembered what she had seen in the Plymouth court-room, it seemed to her that God would surely forgive any lies that served to thwart such knavery!"

By the time of the appeal, Cornelia has no trouble opposing the tactics and philosophy of a government that withholds information from the defense because "the 'secrets' of the Department of Justice were sacred and must be protected!" She agrees with the defense lawyer that "a government which has come to value its own secrets more than it does the lives of its citizens has become a tyranny." Cornelia asks herself a question that echoes through the decades from the 1920s to the 1970s. What does one do when confronted with tyranny on the part of duly elected administrators of government? Can it be, as Vanzetti said, that there is "something fundamentally immoral about the business of dominating the lives of your fellows"?

But Sinclair does not allow Cornelia's rejection of her government's behavior to lead her to Vanzetti's analysis. In Cornelia's final opinion, Vanzetti (for whom

she felt intense motherly love) had ideas that precluded
effective political change:

That was characteristic of all the Boston anarchists—they
were strong on theory, and weak on actuality. . . . No anarchist committee meeting ever ended, because somebody had a
right to say something more; no decision could be taken,
and if it was, it wasn't binding. If you didn't like it, you said
nothing, but went off and worked against it.

So Cornelia reaches Sinclair's balanced and liberal conclusion. Anarchists are simple and charming fanatics
who stand for "the principle, the supremacy of the individual conscience over social compulsion. If the movement produced more dangerous lunatics than it did
prophets and saints, that was the price which humanity
had to pay in the search for higher types of being."

A democratic system, in the liberal view, must be
able and willing to pay this price. When it refuses, when
it risks totalitarianism to avoid anarchy, Cornelia grieves.
Her dismay and frustration is contrasted with Betty's
response to the execution of the Italians. For Betty, who
had worked just as hard to free the men as her grandmother, is exhilarated at their failure:

Don't you see the glory of this case—it kills off the liberals!
Before this it was possible to argue that injustice was an
accident, just an oversight—in a country that was so busy
making automobiles and bathtubs and books of etiquette!
But now here's a test—we settle the question forever! We
take our very best—not merely cheap politicians, but our
great ones! Our biggest business man! Our most cultured
university president! Our supreme court judges—even the
liberal ones! We prove them all alike—they all know what
flag they fight under, who serves out their rations!

Betty and Cornelia join at the end of the book in
turning Sacco and Vanzetti into martyrs. Anarchists

would be able to point to these deaths as illustrations of the inability of well-meaning organizations to free individuals from a hostile class structure. Communists would cite the same case as evidence of the need for radical alternatives to liberal organizations. Cornelia, unable to accept either alternative from the radical left and equally unable to tolerate the status quo, has to opt for something less concrete and much less immediate:

That was what she must manage to realize. Persuade herself that there was a new generation coming, that would care where this one was indifferent; that would count it as something important that two wops had denied themselves happiness so that justice might be born into the world! Think about those young persons of the future; lie here and shut your eyes, and let them come into your presence and speak to you; feel their gentle hands upon your forehead, bidding you to rest, your tense nerves to relax and your heart to stop pounding.

So the 1920s ended with Sinclair still crusading, still hoping for brighter tomorrows, still believing that writers could educate a national mentality, still expressing the liberal dilemma in a critical but sympathetic way. As the nation moved from disillusion to depression, Sinclair's views remained constant. But he experimented widely, trying to find the best means of expression. He maintained an average of at least one novel per year during the 1930s, but none of them seem to be of lasting value or current interest. He wrote a few more plays, but as a dramatist Sinclair *never* had a significant success. So Upton Sinclair's contribution to the great-depression decade is to be remembered primarily by a book on mental telepathy, an autobiography, two rather biographical works, a financial fiasco, and a political campaign that is still being discussed and imitated.

Mental Radio (1930) submits for scientific consideration an extended series of experiments in telepathy that Upton and Craig conducted while he was writing *Boston*. Hundreds of sketches are reproduced, demonstrating Craig's apparent ability to read minds. In an introduction to the book, William McDougall, a Duke University psychologist, contends that the experiments are among the best ever reported.

Consider a typical example. Upton would make nine drawings and put them in nine envelopes. Craig would enter the room, pick up one, concentrate, and attempt to reproduce it. Both original and reproduction would then be printed in *Mental Radio*. Success was, admittedly, far from automatic. In Upton's judgment, out of one series of 290 drawings 65 were total successes, 155 were partially successful, and there were 70 failures. But some of the partial successes are most interesting. Upton draws a fox; Craig draws two guns and a hunting horn. Upton draws a football and proceeds to read a chapter in De Kruif's *Hunger Fighters* about the feeding of cows; Craig draws a football-shaped belly-band placed on a calf.

Craig's facility had both handy and frightening implications. Upton could misplace a plot outline and Craig, with concentration, could tell him where he had put it. On another occasion Craig had the sudden feeling that Jack London was "in terrible mental distress," more extreme than his usual troubled condition. The Sinclairs decided not to go to his ranch without invitation, and within two days London committed suicide.

Sinclair, only too aware that many of his readers would assume that he had discarded reason for mysticism, admitted in *Mental Radio* that he was not comfortable with telepathy. But he had read hundreds of books on the subject, and—most important—he has to believe the evidence with whom he lives. He points out that, when he was a child, the idea that germs can cause disease was considered a superstition. Moreover, he concludes his interest in psychic research was *not* a rejection of rational socialism: "In science, as in politics and religion, it is a lot easier to believe what you have been taught than to set out for yourself and ascertain what happens."

Shortly thereafter, Sinclair ascertained for himself what happens when a socialist tries to play the role of financier. For during all of 1931 and much of 1932 Sinclair was distracted from his own writing by his involvement with another artist's project. Sergei Eisenstein, the famous Russian film director, had come to Hollywood with the intention of combining his genius with American technical facilities to produce movies that would be lasting works of art. But Hollywood paid allegiance to box-office definitions of successful films. So in October of 1930 Eisenstein and Paramount Pictures separated. Rather than returning to the Soviet Union, however, Eisenstein took Charlie Chaplin's suggestion to visit Sinclair in an effort to find adequate financing for a dream film about past and present Mexico.

Sinclair, who had published his opinion about Hollywood in *Oil!*, quickly became interested. He helped raise funds, with the $25,000 goal reached by the end of November. Craig's brother, Hunter Kimbrough, agreed to go along to Mexico as business manager. Russian visas were extended, contracts signed, and the Sinclairs entered a new world of national censorships, international intrigues, and universal frustrations.

The whole affair became incredibly complex.* A movie, *Thunder Over Mexico*, eventually was made, but not according to original plan, ideal, or projected expense. A year after his departure, Eisenstein had already received 175,000 feet of film (to make an eight-thousand-foot movie). But he continued to write for more time, film, and money because the work of art continued to be almost complete. And Sinclair continued to dribble out his resources. He had great difficulty attracting additional money, so he contacted Louella Parsons at Eisenstein's suggestion, and was roundly scolded by Eisenstein for doing so.

Sinclair expended much energy trying to get the Soviet Union to pay royalties for the Sinclair books they had been translating and publishing over the years. This money would be invested in the work of their honored film maker, and the U.S.S.R. would receive free rights to the movie. Instead, the Soviet Union added to Sinclair's troubles. A telegram from Stalin (21 November 1931) informed him that Eisenstein's extended absence from Russia had caused his comrades to consider him a deserter of no more interest to the Soviet Union.

As if this was not enough, Sinclair was receiving a dual set of disaster signals from Mexico. From Kimbrough he learned that Eisenstein had no concept of truth, spent Sinclair's money without regard, shot film as if it were free, disappeared periodically for unexplained reasons, and was working on six or eight movies besides the one contracted. From Eisenstein he learned that an alcoholic Kimbrough divided his time between pursuing prostitutes and frustrating artistic productions. Eisenstein produced signed affidavits to document his

* Harry M. Geduld and Ronald Gottesman have provided a superb edition of pertinent correspondence and documents in *Sergei Eisenstein and Upton Sinclair: The Making & Unmaking of "Que Viva Mexico!"* (Bloomington: Indiana University Press, 1970). This 450-page book provides a chronology, a cast of characters, an annotated bibliography, and excellent editorial comments, with the letters.

charges. Kimbrough wrote to explain how much such affidavits cost on the Mexican market.

In February of 1932 Sinclair again gave his final order to stop the project. It took Eisenstein nineteen days to drive to New York from Laredo. And Sinclair was even more outraged to learn from startled border authorities that, judging from the large collection, a good deal of Eisenstein's time (financed by the still Puritan Sinclair) was spent in making terrifically obscene drawings.

With Craig's health collapsing under the strain, Sinclair would have preferred to sell the problems with the prints. But there were no eager buyers, and the idealistic project deteriorated still further into bickerings about who should edit the film (and where). American communists saw Sinclair as a social fascist determined to degrade revolutionary art. Craig saw American communists as pathological liars eager to imitate their Soviet models. Sinclair saw the movie as an educational experience too expensive to be repeated.

Having had a rather bad year, Sinclair's only significant publication in 1932 was his autobiography, *American Outpost*. In this book, as in his other writings, Sinclair reveals himself to be both honest and egotistical. He points out victories and defeats in his childhood, youth, marriage, and writing career—all based on the general assumption that the study of the life of a genius is both interesting and beneficial.

Over the years, Sinclair had observed much. The updated version of *American Outpost*, published in 1962 as *The Autobiography of Upton Sinclair*, includes an amazing picture of Sinclair, age eighty-four, standing beside a stack of his books that rises higher than he can reach. And should his publications be an inadequate chronicle of ourselves in our times, Sinclair would be delighted to have his readers go through the seven-ton collection of letters and manuscripts now housed in Indiana University's Lilly Library. Sinclair's tax returns are there, open for inspection. So are the little merit badges he received each year from the Southern California Automobile Club for driving his DeSoto safely.

In a way, almost all the books—plus countless letters, articles, and pamphlets—represent Sinclair's effort to tell us what he has experienced. But in at least one case he made a conscious effort to tell someone else's story. *Upton Sinclair Presents William Fox* (1933) outlines in detail the rise and fall of a shrewd capitalist who understood the movie industry much better than Sinclair and lost much more money in it. At Fox's request, Sinclair conducted interviews with Fox lasting hundreds of hours. And although Sinclair has his own reasons for letting readers observe the ethics of high finance, he lets Fox speak for himself, giving us the story as the stenographers took it down.

William Fox, born in Hungary in 1879, was brought to the United States when he was nine months old. Growing up in a Jewish tenement on New York's East Side, in twenty-five years he rose within the entertainment industry to the control of two or three hundred million dollars. This made him important enough to be of interest to Wall Street financiers, but not nearly powerful enough to defeat them. Through manipulations outlined in great detail, Bernard Baruch *et al* seize control of Fox's empire, loot it systematically until it is worth a mere ten million dollars, and leave him talking to a socialist about what happened. Sinclair, of course, has a theory to explain these events, and he adds a few gentle comments at the end of the text suggesting how the economic system might be corrected. Then he makes a graceful exit, stage left, thanking Fox for a fine performance that allows Americans to watch the workings of their economy from the inside.

Sinclair followed this with a major attempt to change those workings from the inside. He had long believed that the economic system could be made democratic through the democratic political process. And, as mentioned above, he had several times run for political office himself. But it was not until 1933 that he devoted his full energy to selling himself as a political practitioner rather than propagandist. He withdrew from the Socialist Party again, but with no mental trauma this time. He simply acknowledged that he continued to be a socialist, that he had always been a democrat, and that socialists and democrats and social democrats were all invited to support his campaign for Governor of California.

With great enthusiasm he published *I, Governor of California and How I Ended Poverty* (1933), outlining the twelve principles of the End Poverty in California (EPIC) movement. These principles included the belief that God had created natural wealth for all to use. In order to apply democracy to economics, Sinclair promised to get rid of sales taxes, increase a steeply graduated income tax, increase inheritance taxes, repeal property tax on homes worth $3000 or less, and provide minimum incomes for all widows and all citizens over sixty years of age. Running against six other Democrats, Sinclair won the majority of the votes cast in the spring primary. Then the campaign began in earnest.

Republican owners of newspapers, who had hoped Sinclair would win the Democratic nomination since he was seen as an easy candidate to defeat, found in Sinclair's publications a gold mine of quotations about divorce and marriage, sex, the church, and especially socialism. Earl Warren, then state chairman of the Republican Party, contended that *the* issue of the campaign was

"Americanism versus radicalism."[17] Harper Knowles, the former Secretary of the Associated Farmers of California, was certain that Sinclair was "the recognized unofficial head 'of the Communist activities in the state.' "[18] And William Jennings Bryan, Jr., formed the League of Loyal Democrats "to save the State from communism, to save the Democratic party from destruction, and to save the New Deal's constructive program."[19]

The results of the election were: Merriam—1,138,000; Sinclair—879,000; Haight—302,000. Within three days Sinclair was writing *I, Candidate for Governor and How I Got Licked* (1935). In this book, which reproduces many of the cartoons published during the fourteen-month campaign, Sinclair once again presented his case against the newspapers as manipulators of the many for the benefit of the few. He also expressed moderate feelings of betrayal. For Franklin D. Roosevelt had suggested to Sinclair that he would make a public statement supporting "production for use," but he never did so.

Outvoted but undefeated, Sinclair went back to his old tool, fiction, to explain to his national audience what he had meant by production for use in California. *Co-op* (1936) is not much of a novel. Fortunately, Sinclair provides a list of his eighty-five characters at the beginning of the book, because they do not tend to stick in the memory. But the novel does convey a picture of the California cooperatives that adopted the traditional idea that good Americans could help themselves out of depressing circumstances.

Sinclair opens the novel, set in 1932, in Pipe City— a part of town in which people live in sewer pipes (five feet in diameter, ten feet long) stored in the vacant lot of the factory manufacturing them. The existence of the citizens of Pipe City is then contrasted with the Italian gardens and polo ponies enjoyed by the elite living next door, and the conclusion of inequity is reached.

Believing that the depression reflects a shortage of money within an abundance of goods, a group of the poor—mostly middle-aged and elderly—decide to return to a barter system. They discover that a farmer will let them grow vegetables on his land if they will cut the dead wood out of his walnut grove. Another rancher will sell cabbage plants wholesale if they will paint his garage. A dealer will provide them with paint if they will do some carpentry for him, and so on. Presenting their skills for exchange, instead of for sale, whenever possible, they find customers.

Musicians and doctors and automobile mechanics and unfriendly infiltrators arrive and make their contributions to a movement that spreads through California. At the end of the novel, having gone through the EPIC effort to make sense of California politics, the defeated leader of the group goes to Washington, D.C., to explain to Roosevelt why self-help is a better plan than the federal programs financed by the New Deal.

In *Co-op*, Sinclair makes much of the excited attitude toward work found in cooperative effort, comparing it with the demeaning effect of "relief" programs. He continued this comparison of labor systems the next year with the publication of *Flivver King*, the unhappy story of Henry Ford's success.

Mixing inventiveness with populist idealism in order to reach the top of America's industrial heap, Sinclair's Ford becomes a slave to his own empire en route. Ironically, a creative thinker who believes in the value of individualism helps change the culture he is trying to preserve by proving that assembly-line production, high wages, and cheap products can create a mass-consumer market.

So although some of Ford's impulses were benevolent, America's economic system entailed production for
profit rather than production for use. Inevitably, Sinclair
argues, Ford has to shoot down his own workers, becoming a fascist as systematically as his Model T's became
part of a middle-class life style.

But if our economic system was wrong, our political
system was still right. And by the end of the 1930s the
existence of the American experiment was again perceived by Sinclair to be under attack from foreign
totalitarian powers. Sinclair, who had been predicting
World War II ever since the end of World War I, set
for himself, at sixty years of age, his last and most ambi-
tious writing project. Keeping himself out of the public
eye for the rest of his life, he attempted to fight the old
battles in a new context through his most extended and
revealing ideological spokesman, Lanny Budd.

5

The All-American Mirror

HAMLET. Be not too tame neither, but let your own dis-
cretion be your tutor: suit the action to the word, the word to
the action; with this special observance, that you o'erstep
not the modesty of nature: for anything so overdone is from
the purpose of playing, whose end, both at the first and now,
was and is, to hold, as 'twere, the mirror up to nature. . . .
—Shakespeare

Eventually comprising what Sinclair considered "the most important part" of his literary production, the Lanny Budd series—proudly identified in Sinclair's *Autobiography* as "eleven volumes, 7,364 pages, over four million words"—sold well, with the first eight novels finding 1,340,139 buyers in the United States alone.[1] Critics, when they deigned to take notice, were not overly impressed. As a reviewer for *Time* concluded: "To the literary, the novels of Upton Sinclair . . . are not literature. To historians, they are not history. To propagandists, they are not propaganda. But to millions of plain people, they are all three of those things."[2] With so many Americans paying attention, the fact that this propaganda for the cause of American liberalism was produced in annual and undiluted doses during a period when this ideology was under extreme stress makes Sinclair a valuable case study of our national psyche and a fine reflector of the times in which he lived.

As observed in Bunny Ross and Cornelia Thornwell, Sinclair's concept of liberalism perceived constant tension between pragmatism—the ability to function effectively in the real world—and the other liberal values that reject totalitarian behavior. The irony is clear and frustrating. Liberal values get suspended "for the duration" of national emergencies because the existence of a nation set up to incorporate liberal values is perceived to be at stake.

Lanny Budd, Sinclair's American liberal, is a self-diagnosed schizophrenic. Seeing himself as caught between his idealism and his definition of realism, he sacrifices the first for the second, fully expecting his acute discomfort to be only temporary and anticipating the American postwar return to normalcy. Most of the series is written within this context. Lanny's conscience is troubled during World War I, during the period between the wars, and during the early years of World War II, by the awareness of his own illiberal behavior. But Lanny knows that he performs functions vital to the interest of a nation that, he believes, will return to the further development of democracy as soon as it is permitted to do so by the totalitarian disturbers of the peace.

To write complete plot synopses of the books in the Lanny Budd series would be to paraphrase the front pages of the newspapers published between World War I and the Korean conflict, adding a central character who is in attendance at most of the significant political events of those decades, who knows the principal characters intimately, who is loved by all, and who influences world history to move in the directions desired by American liberals. A sketchy outline of the territory covered in the series, however, will provide a context for consideration of the way the series reflects the contemporary condition of liberalism. For Lanny, in the opinion of his crusading creator, consistently fights the good fight as American liberals should—reluctantly but well.

World's End (1940) introduces us to a boy who is faced with the apparent collapse of Western civilization. Lanny, born with the twentieth century, is thirteen when the novel begins. The illegitimate son of Robert Budd, an American, Lanny lives in a luxurious villa on the French Riviera with his mother, "Beauty" Budd (neé Mabel Blackless), whom Lanny's father still admires and supports financially.

Money abounds, for the same cynicism that induces Robert Budd to marry respectably while loving a Parisian artist's model permits Robert Budd to manufacture and sell arms to the European practitioners of Machiavellian politics. Thus Lanny prepares himself to enter the world of the idle rich. Quite sober for his age, he

makes a tour of France, Germany, and England just
before World War I, spending the war years in France
and the United States.

With no particular ideology, but with enormous good-
will toward all, Lanny remains neutral throughout the
war, attracted by the developing nationalistic views of
his two best friends, Eric Pomeroy-Nielson (English)
and Kurt Meissner (German). He begins to learn about
frustration:

In wartime it appeared that nobody wanted to see both sides
of any question. . . . Lanny wasn't ever going to become a
Red—he just wanted to hear all sides and understand
them. . . . When the fighting started, he'd be caught between the lines and mowed down.

Through the naive perspective of a strategically
placed American, then, the reader observes the behavior
of historical personages such as Anatole France, Woodrow Wilson, Georges Clemenceau, Adolf Berle, Lloyd
George, T. E. Lawrence, Lincoln Steffens, and Isadora
Duncan.

The novel pays little attention to World War I
itself, concentrating on the effects of that war on people
important to Lanny. Beauty, for example, marries a
French patriot whose face has been burned off in battle.
He dies, and Lanny discovers that his mother has
become the lover of his friend, Kurt, who is fifteen years
younger than she and on the other side of the conflict.
Lanny's personal education regarding the cynical side
of international affairs develops as he is introduced to sex,
at age sixteen, by a British feminist named Rosemary
Codwilliger (pronounced Culliver, Sinclair tells us). This
liberated reader of *Freewoman* loves Lanny with enthusiasm, but when it comes to marriage she prefers British
aristocrats. Lanny's later affair with Gracyn Phillipson,

a poor New England actress, collapses when he discovers that she is willing to pay the sexual price asked of aspiring actresses.

Lanny's love life is not too interesting in itself. But Sinclair used these experiences to illustrate Lanny's introduction to a world in which all ideals are threatened. Sinclair's goal, through Lanny, was to see the state of the world clearly, report events accurately, and then to maintain an idealistic faith in the ability of men to live together harmoniously—somehow. At the end of this beginning novel, Lanny is nineteen. He is made the secretary to Professor Charles T. Alston, one of President Wilson's delegates to the Versailles Conference, the peace conference that was intended to put a stop, once and for all, to international inhumanity and chaos.

Between Two Worlds (1941) documents the failure of the Versailles Conference. Lanny leaves in disgust, but the young idealist will attend many more similar meetings. In fact, during the decade covered by this novel (1919–29), Lanny develops his uncanny ability to be in the important spot at the opportune time. During a visit to Kurt's castle in Silesia, he hears an early speech by Hitler, then known as Adi Schicklgruber. He is in Munich at the time of the Beer Hall *putsch*; he is in New York City when the stock market crashes.

The frugal Lanny has saved enough money of his own to help his father through the immediate financial crisis. In addition, he marries Irma Barnes, the designated heiress to the vast fortunes of J. Paramount Barnes, an American utilities magnate. Irma, while she lasts, will serve as a foil for the maturing Lanny. She will be consistently wrong in all family discussions of racial, sexual, and economic matters.

Beauty Budd, by the way, has married one Parsifal Dingle, a man who can speak directly with God. And

Lanny's uncle, Jesse Blackless, develops as the spokesman for a communist ideology that Lanny understands
but never adopts. Again, the frustrated liberal considers
the tactical advantage of extremist ideologies: "I suppose," says Lanny, "that to be a man of action one has
to be able to see only one side, and be absolutely certain
that it's the whole truth."

Sinclair's next novel, *Dragon's Teeth* (1942), which
was to win the Pulitzer Prize, portrays the situation in
Germany from 1929 to 1934. Lanny, whose social conscience grows in an environment devoid of morality, goes
hunting with Göring, has cocktails with Goebbels, and
attends seances with Sir Basil Zaharoff—Sinclair's personification of a dying capitalism. But, most important,
Lanny discusses the Jewish question with Hitler.

Lanny has a personal interest in the topic, for his
sister is married to the son of Johannes Robin, one of
Germany's most prominent Jews. Johannes, who
becomes symbolic of Jewish wealth used to finance Hitler's rise, believes that his friends in high places will
protect their benefactors. But when his son is sent to
Dachau, the realities of Nazism are clarified for Johannes.
Pretending to convert to Nazism in order to help his
brother-in-law escape, Lanny leaves his playboy period
behind him. His years of ideological fence-sitting provide good cover for the pretended new commitment to
the fascist method of social organization.

Lanny's adventures for the next two years
(1935–37) are presented in *Wide Is the Gate* (1943).
With growing skill as an art broker, Lanny is able to
fascinate the business elites and political leaders of Germany, Spain, France, and England by including tidbits
of inside information along with his negotiations on
paintings. His credibility grows as he manages to bring
a lost Goya out of Spain. Ostensibly visiting with Hitler

(and sell paintings to Herman Göring) at Berchtesgaden, Lanny is really bringing money and priceless information to the anti-Nazi movement and helping victims
escape.

Since the German officials now believe he supports
their cause, they approve of his "pretending" to continue
to be a liberal while in England and France. This proves
confusing to Irma, who understands little of what goes
on, and she delivers an ultimatum. Lanny must quit
fraternizing with socialists or lose her. Sinclair ushers
Irma off the stage via a Reno divorce and has Lanny
secretly marry Trudi Schultz, a radical artist whom he
had helped to escape from Germany. Lanny not only
loves Trudi, he tells her that he would love to be like
her:

You are a saint, Trudi, and a completely integrated per-
sonality. You know exactly what you believe, and it is impossible for you to act or desire to act along any other line.
I imagine it would be hard for you to understand . . . a
person like me, who has been torn since boyhood by two
sets of ideas, two sets of inclinations, two worlds which are
in conflict, and each has a claim upon me and lays hold of
me and pulls.

Conceding this attractive side of single-mindedness,
the whole narrative of *Wide is the Gate* demonstrates
what happens when totalitarian aggressors are appeased
in Europe. As Lanny shuttles back and forth, Hitler
defies the League of Nations by occupying the Rhine-
land, Mussolini invades Ethiopia, and Franco estab-
lishes a successful revolt against the elected government
in Spain.

As the title would imply, *Presidential Agent* (1944)
shows us the same Lanny in a new role. Through Professor Alston, now an active New Dealer, Roosevelt dis-

covers that a curious art broker has access to information available to no other Americans. Designated officially as Number 103, Lanny soon becomes a most valuable dollar-per-year servant of Roosevelt as Sinclair becomes a vigorous supporter of the Democratic administration. In this novel, covering only a period from the summer of 1937 to the Munich agreement of 1938, Lanny relays to Roosevelt trends in the ideas of Hitler, Hess, Göring, and the French Cagoulards—aristocratic conservatives whom Sinclair calls "the Ku Klux Klan of France."

Trudi, who has continued her work in the anti-Nazi resistance in France, is captured by the Germans and imprisoned in a dungeon beneath a château. Lanny attempts a rescue, but he is too late. His wife has already been shipped off to die in Dachau. Lanny decides that he "must hate these Nazis, but it must be a cold and quiet hatred, rationalized and organized, scientific, like their own."

Dragon Harvest (1945), which carries the narrative from the beginning of 1939 to the fall of France in 1940, presents Sinclair's illustration of the dangers of American complacency. Like Lanny, American readers are invited to develop an international perspective. Since Lanny was in Berchtesgaden as Hitler made plans to invade Poland, and since he was again present for the development of German plans to invade England, it is appropriate for the novel to end with Lanny and Hitler in Paris, both contemplating Napoleon's tomb. Like the British, who joined together to rescue their army with the evacuation from Dunkirk, Americans of all classes and ideologies are urged to unify in the national interest.

A World To Win (1946) gives the impression that Sinclair intends for Lanny to win that world single-handedly. He interviews almost everyone of importance. He escapes from French patriots who think he's a Nazi, raising his stock in Germany. He discovers a plot against the life of Roosevelt. He plays Mozart with Einstein who is giving him a crash course on atomic-energy research. He is in Hong Kong on Pearl Harbor day. And he manages to get married again—this time to Laurel Creston, a writer who is also a medium. This virtuoso performance inspired Howard Mumford Jones to call Lanny "a combination of the Count of Monte Cristo, Sherlock Holmes, Harry Hopkins, and the Archangel Raphael."[3]

Lanny continues this indefatigable service in the next volume, *Presidential Mission* (1947). From the spring of 1942 to the spring of 1943 Lanny hops between the White House, where he has automatic and secret access to the Boss, and Europe, where he is bombed in Berlin by the Allies. He scouts North Africa, gets a special pass from Hitler to tour Germany, and takes time out for a vacation with Mrs. Budd and their new baby.

One Clear Call (1948) begins with the 1943 invasion of Sicily and ends with Roosevelt's fourth inauguration. Lanny must study the latest information on rockets and jets so that he can intelligently quiz a secretly anti-Nazi scientist in Germany about German progress in these areas. Himmler finally destroys Lanny's cover, and all his work in Germany must end. But Lanny has learned enough behind the lines to tell General Patton how to take Paris.

The shepherd of *O Shepherd, Speak!* is Roosevelt. Our Secret Agent 103 is worried about the Boss's health as he helps Hopkins draft the Yalta Declaration. But after Roosevelt's death Lanny finds that he can still talk politics with him via a medium. Having been encouraged to persevere under Truman, Lanny watches the atomic bomb test in New Mexico and returns to Germany to help convict Göring at the Nurenberg Trials.

After spending some time tracking down art treasures in Germany—paintings that the Germans stole from occupied lands or bought from Lanny—and after Truman sends Lanny on one last mission to offer Stalin a chance to avoid postwar conflict with America, Lanny decides to devote himself to humanitarian propaganda. A wealthy woman has willed one million dollars to a fund dedicated to the ending of war, and Lanny and Laurel agree that the best way to administer this would be to organize a campaign to avoid World War III. Lanny still sees himself as "one of those unlucky people who have to stand in the middle and get the brickbats from both sides." The series is presumed to be finished.

But in 1953 Sinclair felt obliged to add another volume, *The Return of Lanny Budd*, moving the narrative from 1946 to 1949. Called from his broadcasting job in New Jersey, Lanny is sent to western Europe to check on the spread of counterfeit money by the Soviet Union. He meets his old friend, Kurt Meissner, now a communist, who has literally changed his uniform without altering anything in his ideology. Lanny, who is tortured by the communists in East Germany, discovers that his own sister has become an agent for the Kremlin. And as a propagandist, Lanny is frustrated by a niggardly Congress that fails to support the Voice Of America adequately. In short, Lanny is fighting the new cold war with his old energy, his consistent liberal ideology, and his perpetual reflections on the tribulations of American liberalism in the twentieth century.

There would be debate in his soul; he would suppress it, but it would bob up now and then and come to life. . . . Fiend would inquire, "Have you adopted the doctrine that the end justifies the means?" Conscience would reply, "Can people who deny truth claim the right to truth? Can people use liberty to destroy liberty?" Fiend would jeer, "You sound much like a Communist to me!" The debate would go on for the rest of Lanny's life.

Clearly there is a sense in which Sinclair, through his spokesman, was a remarkably consistent advocate of liberalism. But what sort of consistency is continual schizophrenia? Sinclair's frustrated perception of liberals being pulled to ideological pieces characterizes Lanny throughout the series. As a boy, Lanny was the friend of both German and British nationalists. As the young man described in *Dragon Harvest*,

> there was one half of Lanny Budd—possibly a little more than half—which wanted to quarrel with an evil social order and to make sacrifices in the cause of truth-telling and justice; and there was another half, or near half, which liked to live in a well-appointed home, enjoy well-cooked food, be waited on, have a properly tuned piano. . . .

And as a spy in *Presidential Agent*, "Lanny's job had brought him close to that state known to psychiatrists as schizophrenia; two minds living in the same body."

This conflict, I believe, inheres in the liberal mentality. Personal, immediate, and concrete pressures invite Bunny, Cornelia, and Lanny to make temporary sacrifice of principle for the sake of expediency. But this inconsistency leads to the feelings of guilt suffered by liberals so long as the basic idealism remains. Since this is a complex dilemma, Sinclair's extensive illustration of what happens to Lanny is invaluable.

In *Presidential Agent*, when Trudi is captured by the Nazis, Lanny is ready to risk everything—not to defeat Nazism (merely), but to free the woman he loves. He is, of course, successful in his efforts to defy Nazi security precautions, but with the château successfully entered and the escape route working brilliantly, the person in the torture chamber turns out to be someone else. So

Lanny leaves the victim behind, escaping with his fellow liberators in such a way that the Nazis will never know what had been attempted. He rationalizes his decision in terms of the larger cause: "There wasn't a thing those three intruders could have done; to have carried the man out would have given the whole thing away and ruined the career of a presidential agent." Thus one sacrifices individuals for the good of the larger cause unless those individuals are quite important to one personally. And that larger cause is the preservation of the liberal state a form of government set up to protect the individual.

Another example illustrates what happens to the person who makes this sort of decision too often. Lanny, himself, becomes destroyed as an individual as he hides, in *Presidential Mission*, behind his own sexual morality to avoid taking the relatively small risk involved in saving the life of a German who literally means nothing to him personally. Although he is a professional deceiver of Nazis, he rejects Rosika Diamant's suggestion that he marry her in Germany and thus enable her to avoid the sexual fate reserved for beautiful Jewish women en route to the gas chambers.

Dismissing her suggestion, Lanny says: "I might do what you ask, but as it happens, I have a wife and baby in New York." This is true enough, but the Nazis do not know of his marriage and would not be suspicious. Moreover, Lanny's personal code of honor is not at stake since Rosika makes it clear that she is only interested in saving her own life, assuring him that she will get the "marriage" annulled as soon as they are outside Germany. But Lanny rejects her plan even though Sinclair writes that his response constitutes "what both of them knew was a death sentence."

The implications of this go far beyond the minimal

importance of one character in a set of novels deciding that he does not dare to imperil his larger cause unless he has a personal vested interest—in which case he does so vigorously. The tragic point is that Sinclair cannot imagine his liberal hero acting in any other way, even though Sinclair is aware of what this sort of behavior does to the individual. One of the most touching and despicable scenes in the Lanny Budd novels depicts Lanny's effort to reduce this incident to a joke. Reporting back to the Boss in *Presidential Mission*, Lanny

began to chuckle. "I have stayed too late, but you ought to hear the story of how I was tempted to commit bigamy. Perhaps you will give me permission for that! Or is it in Colonel Donovan's department?"

He told the story of Rosika Diamant, which wasn't really funny but horribly tragic when you stopped to think. Roosevelt laughed first and then he frowned.

I believe that Sinclair refers to Lanny rather than Rosika when he calls the story "tragic." Surely it is the effect upon Lanny, his inability to do what he believes he ought to do, not the probable death of a character we have hardly met, that moves us. I believe that few saw more clearly than Sinclair what was happening to American liberalism, which was not really very funny when you stopped to think. Certainly nobody reflected the frustration of an ideology more extensively that Sinclair—through his spokesman and through his own aging rigidity. Since communism emerges as the variety of totalitarianism that prevents liberals from living like liberals, the easiest way to trace the trek from dilemma to despair is to follow Lanny's changing attitude toward the Soviet Union.

Long after the Moscow purges, Lanny, like most Americans, was glad to have Soviet help at the height of the war against fascist totalitarianism. In *A World To Win* (1945), Stalin appears as a calm and rational leader who tells Lanny confidentially:

The Soviet Union does not want the rest of Europe. The Soviet peoples have all the land and resources they need; they want only peace, so that they can develop what they have. Let the rest of Europe work out its own problems in its own way—subject to but one restriction, that it does not permit itself to be turned into a center of intrigue against the Soviet peoples, such as we saw in the so-called *cordon sanitaire* during the past quarter century.

Two years later, in *One Clear Call*, Sinclair still presents acceptance of Stalin as the difference between conservatives and liberals.

"Winnie is a bulldog and never gives up. He argues, what is the good of winning the war if it leaves Stalin in the Balkans? The Boss [F.D.R.], of course, wants to make friends with Stalin." "That's the difference between a Tory and a democrat," commented Lanny.

But serious doubts are beginning to surface in this book, as Harry Hopkins tells Lanny:

"It appears to be a principle of revolutions that they degenerate, and I fear that Red Russia is no exception. All leaders think about themselves and their own power, and the longer they hold power, the more true that becomes."

By 1953 Sinclair was making public recantations:

It is quite true that in "Presidential Mission" I portrayed Stalin and Mao and had them uttering "quite reasonable views." They were our Allies in the war against Fascism and I believed their promises of peace and world order afterwards. Now I know I was very naive.[4]

So it is not surprising to find that *The Return of Lanny Budd*, published that same year, reveals a spokesman fighting bitterly against the Red Menace. According to Lanny,

The Soviets are on the move. They call themselves internationalists, of course, but every trace of internationalism has gone out of their actions. They are just the old Tsarist imperialists, taking what they can get.

Fortunately, says Lanny, America has the atomic bomb:

if we didn't have it and didn't dangle it the Red Armies would be moving across France today and showering London with a new stock of the V-2 rockets, which the top German scientists are now teaching the Reds to manufacture. It wouldn't be six months more before Stalin would be in Madrid, sitting on the severed head of Franco and thumbing his nose at us.

Of course, there had been a time when Sinclair would have saluted the severer of Franco's head, but since it is now "obvious to all the world that the only thing which had so far kept the Soviet Union from taking possession of Western Europe was that supply of atomic bombs which the United States kept dangling over the Kremlin," Lanny begins to make statements that sound curiously like those uttered by his conservative, munitions-making father early in the series: "I'm not calling for war; on the contrary, I think the only hope of preventing war is for us to rearm and do it quickly, to convince Stalin that he cannot take the rest of the world without war."

It could be for this reason, then, that Sinclair decided that none of his earlier volumes of the series would make appropriate reading for J. Edgar Hoover—one of Sinclair's new allies to whom he wrote on 9 September 1952:

You were kind enough to say that you would be interested to receive one of the "Lanny Budd" books from me. I debated which one to send you, and what I decided was that they are all out of date at present and that what I want you to read is the one I am just completing. This volume is concerned with the Communists and their whole bag of clever tricks.

It is not my purpose here to argue whether or not Sinclair and other liberals were correct to perceive the Soviet Union as an imperialistic threat to America after World War II. And to move from war against Germany and Japan to cold war against Russia can be seen as a consistent liberal resistance to totalitarianism. But Sinclair's description of Lanny portrays only too clearly what happens to liberals when they go to war—using autocratic means to destroy autocrats—for too long. For the hero of Sinclair's final volume is a hard and cynical man, unaware that, in his increasingly monomaniacal efforts to destroy communism, he has simply become a Cornelia who will lie for a cause, a petty combatant for whom no holds are barred.

Early in the book a Treasury agent is dismayed by Lanny's use of Fritz to spy on his own father—Lanny's boyhood friend, Kurt: " 'Mr. Budd,' said the other gravely, 'the Nazis used children to report upon their parents, and the Reds are doing it now. But it is not our practice.' " But Sinclair responded to this by showing how many such tactics were now part of Lanny's weaponry. When Lanny discovers that his sister is a Russian spy, he has the following conversation with his wife:

"It is my plain duty to take it to the FBI."

"Oh, Lanny, how dreadful! Could you bear to do it?"

"Bess herself has given me the authority. You heard her say, 'The individual doesn't matter, only the cause matters.' You and I have a cause, darling."

Sinclair's colleague, Sidney Hook, wrote (9 October 1952) to complain that liberalism should not be presented in quite so illiberal a way:

My only criticism is that you *unnecessarily* make the democrats adopt the kind of immoralism which characterized the Communist outlook. I do not think it is necessary to make Fritz the *son* of Kurt, or Hansi the *husband* of Bess. Your critics will seize upon this to say that you approve tactics that the Stalinists and Nazis use.

But Sinclair was adamant. In a letter to A. P. Biella (29 October 1952) he contended:

It is not merely a question of preserving one's own life, it is a question of preserving modern civilization with its ideals and its humanities. If Lanny has become hard it is because he has seen his ideals betrayed; he has been watching the process for thirty years, all his mature life. Anyhow that is the way I feel about it, and I chose these episodes deliberately for the purpose of saying so.

Thirty years of betrayed ideals, thirty years of perceiving oneself as forced to justify means in terms of ends, thirty years of writing about the frustrations of liberalism—all were too much for an aging Sinclair. The tragedy for American liberalism is reflected only too clearly in the mirror of Upton Sinclair's letter (25 April 1952) to the American Civil Liberties Union:

I've been a Civil Liberties man all my life, but I have to admit that I am having great doubts at the present time of the wisdom in common sense of supporting the Communists in their right to destroy all civil liberties. Every day that I live I discover new evidence of their determination to destroy the civil liberties of all the rest of the world, and I am coming to the conclusion that we ought to take them at their word and abolish their civil liberties before they abolish ours.

Sinclair seems unaware that this statement echoes the position that conservatives had asserted when he had been denied his own civil liberties. For in the days when Sinclair had been demanding rapid social changes, he had been jailed for reading the American Constitution at a time and place deemed subversive by the forces of the status quo.

In fairness, it should be remembered that Sinclair had always put much of his own experience into his work. And these were hard years for him. Craig's health was poor. They tried special diets, temporary moves to Arizona, and devices to take the Los Angeles smog out of their bedrooms. But from 1954 until her death in April of 1961, Sinclair had the care of a beloved patient to add to the cares of a world in which liberalism was not working.

The dependence of Craig and Upton Sinclair upon each other would be hard to exaggerate. In order to relieve the loneliness he was suffering after her death, Sinclair—remembering his wife's advice—determined to find someone to share his last years. Through Hunter Kimbrough he met Mary Hard. After a quiet Episcopal wedding in October of 1961, Sinclair began to enjoy happier years.

In 1962 he received awards from the American Newspaper Guild and the United Auto Workers. Five years later, a week before Mary's death, he was honored by President Johnson at the signing of the Wholesome Meat Act—a law designed to plug loopholes in the original federal legislation that *The Jungle* had inspired. Moreover, many of Sinclair's books were being published and read again.

So the end of Sinclair's *Autobiography*, like the last part of his life, returns to the positive, optimistic sort of attitude that represents Sinclair at his best. As a very old man, he listed ten of his accomplishments that he believed were worth remembering: the federal inspection of domestic meat, the improvement of journalism, the liberalization of the Rockefeller family, the renewed interest in psychic research, the formation of the American Civil Liberties Union, the EPIC effect upon California politics, the spread of democratic ideas in Japan (where his books are popular), the attack upon alcoholism, the introduction of socialism to American colleges, and the history of 1911 to 1950 as recorded in the Lanny Budd novels.

Sinclair served the public, then, as a reflector of the condition of the American liberal by recording what liberals were thinking for half a century—including both optimistic and cynical periods. In terms of his own goal, the production of liberal propaganda, few American authors have been more successful. Certainly his presentation and personification of the complex liberal dilemma remains the most exhaustive analysis on record.

When he died in a New Jersey nursing home in the autumn of 1968, America lost a crusader who deserves international recognition for his tireless efforts to educate a national public. And that recognition may be forthcoming, for Sinclair's ideas were not buried when he died.

Michael Harrington, for example, had advanced an argument for socialism that simply paraphrases Sinclair's social-democratic thought:

I think the argument for American socialism must be made in specifically American terms, i.e., with the understanding that any possibility for mass Socialist consciousness must emerge out of the present liberal consciousness. Socialism must, therefore, be put as a logical next step for liberalism, indeed as the only way to assure the actual achievement of liberal values. This is not only good rhetorical strategy; it also accurately describes the only way socialism can possibly become a serious political movement in America.[5]

And some Canadians, at least, are taking Sinclair's politics quite seriously. Nobody knows, at present, what the eventual impact of the New Democratic Party will be in Canada. But in 1972 they ended the twenty-year rule of the Social Credit Party in British Columbia. And their leader, David Barrett (whose father had been a member of the I.W.W. during the great depression), gave credit where due: "We're the culmination of Upton Sinclair's struggle in California, 50 years later."[6]

If his suspicion that some sort of soul-consciousness continues to exist after death is correct, then somewhere the spirit of Sinclair is smiling. For years before, in *The Brass Check*, Upton Sinclair had predicted: "Mankind will not consent to be lied to indefinitely."

Notes

1. The Problem

1. Edmund Wilson, "Lincoln Steffens and Upton Sinclair," *New Republic* 72 (28 September 1932) :174.
2. Upton Sinclair, *My Lifetime in Letters* (Columbia, Missouri, 1960), p. 167.
3. Ibid., p. 353.
4. George Orwell, *The Road to Wigan Pier* (London, 1965), p. 184.
5. Granville Hicks, "Warmakers and Peacemakers," *New Republic* 102 (24 June 1940) :863.
6. Granville Hicks, "The Survival of Upton Sinclair," *College English* 4 (January 1943) :214.
7. Malcolm Cowley, "Man of Good Will," *New Republic* 108 (11 January 1943) :58.
8. J. D. Koerner, "The Last of the Muckrake Men," *South Atlantic Quarterly* 55 (April 1956) :221, 222.
9. Floyd Dell, *Upton Sinclair: A Study in Social Protest* (New York, 1927), p. 11. In his appendix to *O Shepherd, Speak!* Sinclair reported that within three months of publication in Japan the sales of *Dragon's Teeth* approached the seven-year total in the United States.

10. "Sinclair's War & Peace," *Time* 35 (24 June 1940):92.
11. George J. Becker, "Upton Sinclair: Quixote in a Flivver," *College English* 21 (December 1959):135.
12. Irving Howe, *Politics and the Novel* (New York, 1957), p. 20.
13. Sinclair, *My Lifetime in Letters*, p. 61.
14. M. H. Abrams, *The Mirror and the Lamp: Romantic Theory and the Critical Tradition* (New York, 1953), p. 15.
15. Ibid.
16. H. Wayne Morgan, *American Socialism, 1900–1960* (Englewood Cliffs, New Jersey, 1964), pp. 2, 3.
17. Donald Drew Egbert, *Socialism and American Art* (Princeton, New Jersey, 1967), p. 107.
18. Ibid., p. 130.

2.   The Preparation

1. Quoted by Floyd Dell, *Upton Sinclair*, p. 45. This joke was one of many collected in a scrapbook by Sinclair's mother.
2. Floyd Dell, *Upton Sinclair*, p. 47.
3. Richard Le Gallienne, quoted by Dell, *Upton Sinclair*, p. 86.

3.   The Muckraker

1. Samuel E. Morrison and Henry Steele Commager, *The Growth of the American Republic*, 2 (New York, 1950): 910.
2. Maldwyn A. Jones, *American Immigration* (Chicago, 1960), p. 202.
3. Oscar Handlin, *The Uprooted* (New York, 1951), p. 61.
4. Ibid., p. 76.
5. John Higham, *Strangers in the Land* (New York, 1967), p. 135.

6. Quoted by Richard Hofstadter, *Social Darwinism in American Thought* (Boston, 1955), p. 45.
7. Hofstadter, *The Age of Reform* (New York, 1955), p. 194.
8. Ibid., p. 187.
9. *New York Times*, 5 June 1906, p. 2, col. 7.
10. J. Ogden Armour, "The Packers and the People," *Saturday Evening Post* 178 (10 March 1906) :6.
11. *New York Times*, 4 May 1906, p. 8, col. 8.
12. Quoted by *New York Times*, 29 May 1906, p. 2, col. 2. For an article supporting Sinclair's point of view and providing excellent photographs of the stockyards, slaughtering process, and housing of workers see W. K. Jaques, "A Picture of Meat Inspection," *The World's Work* (May 1906), pp. 7491–7505.
13. Letter from Sinclair to Mr. and Mrs. Gaylord Wilshire (28 June [1909]), quoted by Howard H. Quint, "Upton Sinclair's Quest for Artistic Independence—1909," *American Literature* 29 (1957–58) :196.
14. Ibid., p. 195.
15. *New York Times*, 7 October 1906, pt. 3, p. 2, col. 1–5. See also 10 May 1906, p. 5, col. 2 for an extended outline of the goals of the colony.
16. *New York Times*, 10 August 1906, p. 5, col. 2.
17. *New York Times*, 24 August 1911, p. 1, col. 5.

4. The Perpetual Progressive

1. Walter Rideout, *The Radical Novel in the United States* (New York, 1966), p. 32.
2. *New York Times*, 8 July 1914, p. 6, col. 2.
3. For endorsement of his plan by Maxim Gorky as well as criticisms from Israel Zangwill, Peter Kropotkin, and George Bernard Shaw see *My Lifetime in Letters*, pp. 56, 106–110.
4. *Chicago Tribune*, 22 July 1917, part VII, p. 5, col. 2.

5. Quoted by Floyd Dell, *Upton Sinclair*, p. 150.

6. *New York Times*, 10 November 1922, p. 19, col. 2.

7. *New York Times*, 21 April 1923, p. 13, col. 4.

8. *New York Times*, 17 May 1923, p. 20, col. 3–4.

9. Frederick J. Hoffman, *The Twenties* (New York, 1965), p. 427.

10. Sinclair, "Poor Me and Pure Boston," *Nation* 124 (29 June 1927) :713.

11. Their plan is modeled on a similar school called "Commonwealth" in Mena, Arkansas. See Sinclair's letter to the editor of *Saturday Review* (16 July 1927) :980.

12. Sherman Paul, *Edmund Wilson* (Urbana, Illinois, 1965), p. 93.

13. Walter Rideout, *The Radical Novel in the United States*, pp. 133–134.

14. Edmund Wilson, *The Shores of Light* (New York, 1952), p. 496.

15. Louis Joughin and Edmund M. Morgan, *The Legacy of Sacco and Vanzetti* (Chicago, 1964), p. 448.

16. Ibid., p. 510.

17. Clarence F. McIntosh, "Upton Sinclair and the EPIC Movement," (unpublished dissertation, Stanford University, 1955), p. 226.

18. *New York Times*, 27 October 1938, p. 10. col. 3.

19. McIntosh, pp. 227–228. For discussion of the firm hired to create the false picture of Sinclair as a communist see Irwin Ross, "The Supersalesmen of California Politics: Whitaker and Baxter," *Harper's Magazine* 219 (July 1959) :55–61.

5. *The All-American Mirror*

1. *Time* 52 (6 September 1948) :90.

2. *Time* 35 (24 June 1940) :92.

3. Howard Mumford Jones, *Atlantic Monthly* 178 (August 1946) :150.

4. "Upton Sinclair Answers His Critics," *London Forward*, 17 January 1953, p. 1, col. 6.
5. Michael Harrington, "Say What You Mean—Socialism," *Nation* 218 (25 May 1974) :651.
6. Quoted by Derek Shearer, "British Columbia: Socialism in One Province," *Ramparts* 12 (February 1974) :23.

Bibliography

1. Selected Works by Upton Sinclair

FICTION

Springtime and Harvest. New York: The Sinclair Press, 1901.
Reissued as *King Midas.* New York: Funk & Wagnalls,
1901.
Prince Hagen. Boston: L. C. Page, 1903.
Manassas. New York: Macmillan, 1904.
The Jungle. New York: Doubleday, Page, 1906.
The Overman. New York: Doubleday, Page, 1907.
The Metropolis. New York: Moffat, Yard, 1908.
The Moneychangers. New York: B. W. Dodge, 1908.
Samuel the Seeker. New York: B. W. Dodge, 1910.
Love's Pilgrimage. New York: Mitchell Kennerley, 1911.
Sylvia. Philadelphia: John C. Winston, 1913.
Damaged Goods [based on drama, *Les Avariés*, by Eugène
Brieux]. Philadelphia: John C. Winston, 1913.
Sylvia's Marriage. Philadelphia: John C. Winston, 1914.
King Coal. New York: Macmillan, 1917.
Jimmie Higgins. New York: Boni and Liveright, 1919.
100%: The Story of a Patriot. Pasadena: The Author, 1920.

They Call Me Carpenter. New York: Boni and Liveright, 1922.

Oil! New York: A. & C. Boni, 1927.

Boston. New York: A. & C. Boni. 1928.

Mountain City. New York: A. & C. Boni. 1930.

Roman Holiday. New York: Farrar and Rinehart, 1931.

The Wet Parade. New York: Farrar and Rinehart, 1931.

Co-op. New York: Farrar and Rinehart, 1936.

The Gnomobile. New York: Farrar and Rinehart, 1936.

The Flivver King. Pasadena: The Author, 1937.

No Pasaran! Pasadena: The Author, 1937.

Little Steel. New York: Farrar and Rinehart, 1938.

Our Lady. Emmaus, Pennsylvania: Rodale Press, 1938.

World's End. New York: Viking, 1940.

Between Two Worlds. New York: Viking, 1941.

Dragon's Teeth. New York: Viking, 1942.

Wide Is the Gate. New York: Viking, 1943.

Presidential Agent. New York: Viking, 1944.

Dragon Harvest. New York: Viking, 1945.

A World To Win. New York: Viking, 1946.

Presidential Mission. New York: Viking, 1947.

One Clear Call. New York: Viking, 1948.

O Shepherd, Speak! New York: Viking, 1949.

Another Pamela. New York: Viking, 1950.

The Return of Lanny Budd. New York: Viking, 1953.

What Didymus Did. London: Allan Wingate, 1954. Reissued as *It Happened To Didymus*. New York: Sagamore, 1958.

Theirs Be the Guilt [revision of *Manassas*]. New York: Twayne, 1959.

Affectionately Eve. New York: Twayne, 1961.

NONFICTION WRITINGS

A Captain of Industry. Girard, Kansas: Appeal to Reason, 1906.

The Industrial Republic. New York: Doubleday, Page, 1907.

Good Health and How We Won It [with Michael Williams]. New York: Frederick A. Stokes, 1909.

The Fasting Cure. New York: Mitchell Kennerley, 1911.

The Profits of Religion. Pasadena: The Author, 1918.

The Brass Check. Pasadena: The Author, 1920.

The Book of Life: Mind and Body. New York: Macmillan, 1921.

The Book of Life: Love and Society. Pasadena: Sinclair-Paine, 1922.

The Goose-step. Pasadena: The Author, 1923.

The Goslings. Pasadena: Upton Sinclair, 1924.

Mammonart. Pasadena: The Author, 1925.

Letters to Judd. Pasadena: Upton Sinclair, 1926.

Money Writes. New York: A. & C. Boni, 1927.

Mental Radio. Monrovia, California: The Author, 1930.

Upton Sinclair Presents William Fox. Los Angeles: The Author, 1933.

I, Governor of California, and How I Ended Poverty. New York: Farrar and Rinehart, 1933.

The Way Out—What Lies Ahead for America? New York: Farrar and Rinehart, 1933.

EPIC Plan for California. New York: Farrar and Rinehart, 1934.

An Upton Sinclair Anthology, compiled by I. O. Evans. New York: Farrar and Rinehart, 1934.

I, Candidate for Governor, and How I Got Licked. Pasadena: The Author, 1935.

What God Means to Me. New York: Farrar and Rinehart, 1936.

Terror in Russia? Two Views [with Eugene Lyons]. New York: Richard R. Smith, 1938.

Expect No Peace! Girard, Kansas: Haldeman-Julius, 1939.

A Personal Jesus. New York: Evans, 1952.

The Cup of Fury. Great Neck, New York: Channel, 1956.

DRAMA

Plays of Protest. New York: Mitchell Kennerley, 1912.

Hell. Pasadena: The Author, 1923.

The Millennium. Pasadena: Upton Sinclair, 1924.

The Pot Boiler. Girard, Kansas: Haldeman-Julius, 1924.
Singing Jailbirds. Pasadena: Upton Sinclair, 1924.
Bill Porter. Pasadena: The Author, 1925.
Depression Island. Pasadena: The Author, 1935.
Wally for Queen! Pasadena: Upton Sinclair, 1936.
Marie Antoinette. New York: Vanguard, 1939.
A Giant's Strength. Monrovia, California: The Author, 1948.
The Enemy Had It Too. New York: Viking, 1950.

AUTOBIOGRAPHY

American Outpost. New York: Farrar and Rinehart, 1932.
The Autobiography of Upton Sinclair. New York: Harcourt, Brace & World, 1962.

LETTERS

Sergei Eisenstein and Upton Sinclair: The Making & Unmaking of "Que Viva Mexico!" edited by Harry M. Geduld and Ronald Gottesman. Bloomington: Indiana University, 1970.
My Lifetime In Letters. Columbia: University of Missouri, 1960.

2.   Works on Upton Sinclair

BIBLIOGRAPHICAL SOURCES

Gottesman, Ronald. *A Catalogue of Books, Manuscripts, and Other Materials from the Upton Sinclair Archives.* Bloomington, Indiana: Lilly Library, 1963.
———. *Upton Sinclair: An Annotated Checklist.* Kent, Ohio: Kent State University, 1973.
———, and Charles L. P. Silet. *The Literary Manuscripts of Upton Sinclair.* Columbus: Ohio State University, 1972.

GENERAL BACKGROUND WORKS

Aaron, Daniel. *Writers on the Left.* New York: Avon, 1969.

Blotner, Joseph. *The Modern American Political Novel.* Austin: University of Texas, 1966.

Brown, Deming. *Soviet Attitudes Toward American Writing.* Princeton: Princeton University, 1962.

Chalmers, David Mark. *The Social and Political Ideas of the Muckrakers.* New York: Citadel, 1964.

Egbert, Donald Drew. *Socialism and American Art.* Princeton: Princeton University, 1967.

French, Warren. *The Social Novel At The End of An Era.* Carbondale: Southern Illinois University, 1966.

Gilbert, James Burkhart. *Writers and Partisans: A History of Literary Radicalism in America.* New York: John Wiley and Sons, 1968.

Harrington, Michael. *Toward A Democratic Left.* Baltimore: Penguin, 1969.

Hartz, Louis. *The Liberal Tradition in America.* New York: Harcourt, Brace & World, 1955.

Hicks, Granville. *The Great Tradition.* New York: Macmillan, 1933.

Hofstadter, Richard. *The Age of Reform.* New York: Vintage, 1955.

———. *Social Darwinism in American Thought.* Boston: Beacon, 1955.

Howe, Irving. *Politics and the Novel.* New York: Horizon, 1957.

Josephson, Matthew. *The Robber Barons.* New York: Harcourt, Brace, 1934.

Kazin, Alfred. *On Native Grounds.* New York: Reynal & Hitchcock, 1942.

Morgan, H. Wayne. *American Socialism, 1900–1960.* Englewood Cliffs, New Jersey: Prentice-Hall, 1964.

Rideout, Walter, B. *The Radical Novel in the United States 1900–1954.* New York: Hill and Wang, 1956.

BIOGRAPHICAL WORKS

Dell, Floyd. *Upton Sinclair: A Study in Social Protest.* New York: George H. Doran, 1927.

Harris, Leon. New York: Holt, Rinehart and Winston, in preparation.

Harte, James L. *This Is Upton Sinclair.* Emmaus, Pennsylvania: Rodale, 1938.

Larsen, Charles E. "The EPIC Campaign of 1934." *Pacific Historical Review* 27 (May 1958) :127–147.

McIntosh, Clarence Frederic. "Upton Sinclair and the EPIC Movement." Ph.D. dissertation, Stanford University, 1955.

McWilliams, Carey. "Upton Sinclair and his E.P.I.C." *New Republic* 80 (22 August 1934) :39–41.

Quint, Howard H. "Upton Sinclair's Quest for Artistic Independence—1909." *American Literature* 29 (May 1957) : 194–202.

Remley, David. "The Correspondence of H. L. Mencken and Upton Sinclair: 'An Illustration of How Not to Agree'." Ph.D. dissertation, Indiana University, 1967.

Sinclair, Mary Craig. *Southern Belle.* New York: Crown, 1957.

Soderbergh, Peter A. "Upton Sinclair and Hollywood." *Midwest Quarterly* 11 (Winter 1970) :173–191.

Zanger, Martin. "Politics of Confrontation: Upton Sinclair and the Launching of the ACLU in Southern California." *Pacific Historical Review* 38 (November 1969) : 383–406.

CRITICAL WORKS

Ainsworth, Ed. "Remembering 'Uppie'." *Saturday Review of Literature* 50 (30 September 1967) :32–33.

Becker, George J. "Upton Sinclair: Quixote in a Flivver." *College English* 21 (December 1959) :133–140.

Brooks, Van Wyck. *Sketches in Criticism.* New York: Dutton, 1932.

Cantwell, Robert. "Upton Sinclair." In *After the Genteel Tradition*, ed. Malcolm Cowley. Carbondale: Southern Illinois, 1964.

Cowley, Malcolm. "Man of Good Will." *New Republic* 108 (11 January 1943) :58.

Downs, Robert B. Afterword to *The Jungle*. New York: New American Library, 1960.

Duram, James C. "Upton Sinclair's Realistic Romanticism." *University Studies* (Wichita State), May 1970, pp. 1–11.

Hicks, Granville. "The Survival of Upton Sinclair." *College English* 4 (January 1943) :213–220.

Joughin, Louis and Edmund M. Morgan. *The Legacy of Sacco and Vanzetti*. Chicago: Quadrangle, 1964.

Koerner, J. D. "The Last of the Muckrake Men." *South Atlantic Quarterly* 55 (April 1956) : 221–232.

Swados, Harvey. "The World of Upton Sinclair." *Atlantic Monthly* 208 (December 1961) : 96, 98, 100, 102.

Van Doren, Carl. *Contemporary American Novelists*. New York: Macmillan, 1922.

Yoder, Jon A. "Upton Sinclair, Lanny, and the Liberals." *Modern Fiction Studies*, in preparation.

Index